Par 3
Tea-Time at the MASTERS®

Relaxed Entertaining Augusta, Georgia Style

JUNIOR LEAGUE OF AUGUSTA, GEORGIA

THE OFFICIAL COOKBOOK SERIES FOR
THE CITY OF AUGUSTA, GEORGIA

CREATORS OF

TEA-TIME AT THE MASTERS® *AND*
SECOND ROUND, TEA-TIME AT THE MASTERS®

Par 3
Tea-Time at the MASTERS®

Relaxed Entertaining Augusta, Georgia Style

JUNIOR LEAGUE OF AUGUSTA, GEORGIA

Par 3 Tea-Time at the MASTERS®
Relaxed Entertaining Augusta, Georgia Style

The Junior League of Augusta, Georgia, is an organization of women committed to promoting voluntarism, developing the potential of women, and improving the community through the effective action and leadership of trained volunteers. Its purpose is exclusively educational and charitable.

The golfing history excerpts highlighted throughout this book were taken, with permission, from the following: the *Masters® Annuals,* the *Masters® Journals,* and the *Masters® Media Guide;* published by the Augusta National Golf Club; www.masters.org; and *The Making of the Masters,* by David Owen, copyright © 1999, Simon & Schuster.

The Junior League of Augusta, Georgia, gratefully acknowledges the significant contribution of Augusta National, Inc., to the success of the Tea-Time at the Masters® series of cookbooks. The proceeds have supported many charitable projects in our community since 1977.

Par 3 Tea-Time at the MASTERS®
PUBLISHED BY JUNIOR LEAGUE OF AUGUSTA, GEORGIA

Copyright © 2005 by
Junior League of Augusta, Georgia
P. O. Box 40058
Augusta, Georgia 30909
706-736-0033

This cookbook is a collection of favorite recipes, which are not necessarily original recipes.

Food Photography © Junior League of Augusta

Library of Congress Control Number: 2005921370
ISBN: 0-9621062-5-9

Edited, Designed, and Manufactured by
Favorite Recipes® Press
an imprint of

FRP

P. O. Box 305142
Nashville, Tennessee 37230
800-358-0560

Art Director: Steve Newman
Book Design: Starletta Polster Design
Project Editor: Nicki Pendleton Wood

Manufactured in the United States of America
First Printing: 2005
25,000 copies

The word "MASTERS®" is registered in the U.S. Patent and Trademark Office as a trademark and service mark of Augusta National, Inc., Augusta, Georgia.

In Dedication

In 1974, a small group of Junior League of Augusta volunteers conceived an idea for a cookbook fund-raiser. That book, *Tea-Time at the Masters*®, was born in 1977. Little did those women know at the time that they had created a legacy that would span thirty years of fund-raising for our community.

Their winning combination of golf lore and can't-miss cooking led to the launch of a second book, *Second Round, Tea-Time at the Masters*®, in 1988. The books were so successful that Tea-Time Publications, Inc., was formed.

The success can only be owned by all of the dedicated women of the Junior League of Augusta, Georgia, who have committed to and supported these two projects beginning more than thirty years ago. That woman is titled a sustainer. A sustainer, by definition, is someone who stands the test of time, who upholds her commitment, who is steadfast, who maintains her ideals, who supports.

The cause of these sustainer members has heralded the projects of the Junior League into the new century. Their insight and dedication have enabled the Junior League of Augusta to publish a third book in the Tea-Time at the Masters® series, without sponsorship dollars. The committee is proud to follow in their footsteps and is overwhelmed by their enthusiasm and devotion. We thank them for their legacy, their advice, and their fortitude. We dedicate this third and final book in the series to them.

Reflections from Barbara Nicklaus

Cookbooks are my passion. I love to cook, and I have a fantastic collection of cookbooks. However, if you skimmed through my collection, you would immediately find out that my favorite and most-used books are *Tea-Time at the Masters®* and *Second Round Tea-Time at the Masters®*. Some of the pages have so many spots on them, you can hardly read the ingredients. So, it is an honor and a privilege to be a part of *Par 3 Tea-Time at the Masters®*—the final book in the series.

Entertaining seems to be more casual and relaxed these days, and we all want recipes and/or menus that will allow us to entertain our guests as well as be able to spend more time with them and less time in the kitchen.

That paragraph probably exemplifies Masters week for our family. After spending the days at Augusta National, I am always looking for quick, but wonderful, menus. I never know if there will be six or twenty people for dinner on any given night, because Jack loves to have friends and family join us. *Par 3 Tea-Time at the Masters®* will be a great guide in helping you (and me) plan these memorable times.

Masters week is a special one for Jack and me, and we will always consider Augusta our "home away from home." We both still get chills when we drive down Magnolia Lane, and the endearment that the Masters and Augusta have shown Jack will be a treasure forever.

Jack's mom and dad came with us to Jack's first Masters in 1959. His dad continued to be there each year until his death, but his mother had never returned. One year she mentioned to us that she would like to see one more Masters. Isn't it ironic that she picked 1986 to join us? That was Jack's last and probably most memorable Masters victory. And what made it even more special was that he had our eldest son, Jack Jr., by his side for those seventy-two precious holes! What a thrill for me, as a wife and mother, to see Jack and Jackie walk off the eighteenth green that Sunday afternoon with their arms around each other, both shedding tears of joy. That was definitely one of my most memorable Augusta experiences.

"There is magic in a successful blend of flavors, flowers, and favorite companions. The perfect combination repeated once is a gift, more often than that a tradition." The carefully planned menus that follow were chosen to help create those magical and memorable experiences we all seek to enrich our lives. I hope many of these menus will become traditions in your home.

Thanks to the Junior League of Augusta for the educational and charitable work that the members perform to promote voluntarism. How fitting that the proceeds from *Par 3 Tea-Time at the Masters®* will be used to support the league's projects within the community.

Please enjoy the entire contents of this special cookbook, and always remember to cook with love!

Barbara

Golf legend and Augusta National co-founder Bobby Jones instructed that a "par 3 should be a test of precision, not of strength."

In *Par 3 Tea-Time at the Masters®*, the menus and recipes are designed to allow you to "play with precision" when you cook and entertain. Present fabulous food and atmosphere with "Augusta, Georgia style" and be ready to relax and enjoy your occasion when guests arrive.

The success of the Masters® Golf Tournament and the beauty of the grounds at the Augusta National Golf Club are attributed to the vision and attention to detail of founders Clifford Roberts and Robert Tyre Jones, Jr. In the tradition of *Tea-Time at the Masters®* and *Second Round, Tea-Time at the Masters®*, *Par 3* has done the behind-the-scenes preparation—providing unique party themes, spectacular food, and ideas for preparing ahead.

As visitors to Augusta each spring understand, an event need not be formal to be special. Par 3 Day is one to delight in the beauty of the landscape, guarded by stately pines—admiring azaleas; gathering around the practice greens; hoping for an autograph as a favorite golfer exits the driving range; and lining the Par 3 course for the Par 3 Contest, where sons and daughters caddie for their fathers and competitors enjoy each other's company.

Relaxed Entertaining Augusta, Georgia Style offers insight into the special flair found in Augusta's celebrations, both during Masters® Tournament week and other occasions throughout the year. We are certain that you will find new favorite recipes among our menus and will enjoy the diversity of tastes and occasions gathered from those who call Augusta, Georgia, home— year-round, or for one memorable week each April.

Table of Contents

After the
Par 3 Party 12

Picnicking at
Georgia Golf
Hall of Fame's
Botanical
Gardens,
A Springtime
Outing 22

Cooking with
Friends 30

Christening
Celebration
Luncheon 38

"Nach-O"
Ordinary
Birthday Party 48

Cruising on the
Augusta Canal,
A Sunset Supper 60

Summer
Supper Club 66

Engagement
Cocktail Party 74

Mix-and-Match
Brunch for
Weekend
Houseguests 82

Table of Contents

Lounging at the Lake, A Family Fourth of July 92

Date Night Dinner for Two 100

Back-to-School Bash 106

Strolling Through Summerville, A Progressive Dinner 112

Fall Fireside Supper 124

HOLIDAY DESSERT
BUFFET 130

FESTIVE FAMILY
CHRISTMAS EVE 142

GATHERING FOR THE
AUGUSTA FUTURITY,
A DOWN-HOME
BARBECUE 150

CHAMPIONS
DINNER 160

THE 19TH HOLE 168

Cookbook Development Committee 198
Special Acknowledgments 199
Contributors 200
Index 202

After the Par 3 Party

Mustard-Marinated Shrimp
Spicy Red Bell Pepper Dip
Kahlúa Pecan Brie
Honey-Gingered Pork Tenderloin
Couscous-Stuffed Portobello Mushrooms
Zesty Carrots
Marinated Garden Salad
Lime Cake

Wednesday of Masters® Tournament Week has to be the favorite day for entertaining in Augusta, Georgia. It is the last day for choosing pre-tournament favorites and the final day for patrons to carry cameras on the scenic grounds. Competitors and their fans share in the camaraderie of the Par 3 Contest, which is held on the designated Par 3 course, adjacent to the Club House at the Augusta National Golf Club.

The Par 3 Contest is an opportunity for golfers to sharpen their short game before the tournament begins on Thursday, and spectators are privileged to closeup views of their favorite competitors, as well as many spectacular shots. Since the Par 3 Contest began in 1960, there have been fifty-five holes-in-one, a record five in 2002. Golf fans know that no player has ever won the Par 3 Contest and the Masters® Tournament in the same year—perhaps this year that will change.

The After the Par 3 Party menu is to be prepared in advance so that you can come off the golf course and relax while hosting a party later that day. Even if you have houseguests, the Mustard-Marinated Shrimp and Spicy Red Bell Pepper Dip are ready to serve when you arrive home. Last minute details include baking the Kahlúa Pecan Brie and the vegetables and grilling the pork tenderloin.

The key to a relaxed, successful party is to plan in advance. Be ahead of the game by setting the buffet table and preparing the tabletop decorations several days before your event. One tip for arranging an inviting, interesting buffet is to elevate foods to different levels. Place boxes, risers, or plant stands underneath the tablecloth—use anything that will keep each dish sturdy. Composing these pedestals underneath certain dishes lends a professional, sophisticated look to your table.

Arrange flowers readily available from your garden, or, for an easy tabletop decoration, an attractive container or planter filled with mondo grass with gently placed golf balls carries the theme of the day.

Mustard-Marinated Shrimp

2 quarts water
1 lemon, quartered
1 garlic clove, crushed
1 package shrimp/crab boil
2 1/2 pounds deveined peeled shrimp
1/4 cup tarragon vinegar
1/4 cup red wine vinegar
1/4 cup dry mustard
1 teaspoon black pepper

1 teaspoon red pepper flakes
2 teaspoons salt
1/4 cup vegetable oil
1/4 cup extra-virgin olive oil
1/4 cup finely chopped parsley
2 garlic cloves, pressed
6 green onions, sliced
1/4 cup drained capers
Crackers and chilled cucumber slices

◆ Combine the water, lemon, crushed garlic and shrimp boil in a large saucepan. Bring to a boil and let simmer for 5 to 10 minutes to blend the flavors. Add the shrimp and remove from the heat. Let stand until the shrimp turn pink. Drain and let cool.

◆ Whisk the tarragon vinegar, wine vinegar, dry mustard, black pepper, red pepper flakes and salt in a large bowl. Whisk in the vegetable oil and olive oil slowly. Whisk until the mixture thickens slightly. Stir in the parsley, pressed garlic, green onions and capers. Add the shrimp and stir to coat. Cover and chill overnight. Remove the shrimp from the marinade to a serving dish. Discard the marinade. Serve with wooden picks or with crackers and chilled cucumber slices.

Excellent for a buffet or as a first course.

SERVES 10

Spicy Red Bell Pepper Dip

1 small red onion, peeled
1 teaspoon olive oil
1 (7-ounce) jar roasted red peppers, drained
12 fresh basil leaves, or 1/2 teaspoon dried basil
12 ounces cream cheese, softened
2 tablespoons prepared horseradish

3/4 teaspoon salt
1/4 teaspoon cayenne pepper
Red and green bell peppers, cut into strips
Mushrooms, halved
Grape tomatoes
Asparagus spears, blanched
Bagel chips

◆ Preheat the oven to 400 degrees. Place the onion in a small baking dish. Drizzle with the olive oil. Bake for 45 minutes or until soft. Let cool. Purée the onion, roasted peppers and basil in a food processor. Add the cream cheese and process just until combined. Remove to a bowl and stir in the horseradish, salt and cayenne. Cover and chill for at least 3 hours.
◆ Place the bowl of dip in the center of a serving platter. Surround with bell pepper strips, mushroom halves, tomatoes, asparagus spears and bagel chips.

The arranged vegetables create a splashy presentation.

SERVES 12

Kahlúa Pecan Brie

3/4 cup finely chopped pecans
3/4 cup packed brown sugar
1/4 cup Kahlúa

1 (14- to 16-ounce) whole miniature
    Brie cheese
Assorted crackers

◆ Spread the pecans in a 9-inch glass pie plate. Microwave on High for 4 to 6 minutes or until toasted, stirring every 2 minutes. Add the brown sugar and Kahlúa and stir to mix well.
◆ Remove the rind from the top of the Brie and place the cheese in a small baking dish. Spoon the pecan mixture evenly over the Brie.
◆ Bake at 350 degrees for 15 to 20 minutes. Serve with assorted crackers.

SERVES 14

THE "BIG OAK TREE" ON THE GOLF COURSE SIDE OF THE CLUBHOUSE IS A LIVE OAK, PLANTED WHEN THE BUILDING WAS COMPLETED IN THE LATE 1850S. THE "BIG OAK" IS ONE OF THE FAVORITE GATHERING PLACES DURING THE MASTERS® TOURNAMENT.

Honey-Gingered Pork Tenderloin

4 pork tenderloins
  (4 to 4^1/$_2$ pounds total)

^{1}/$_2$ cup honey

^{2}/$_3$ cup soy sauce

^{1}/$_2$ cup water

^{1}/$_4$ cup packed brown sugar

2^1/$_2$ tablespoons minced fresh ginger

2 tablespoons minced garlic

2 tablespoons ketchup

^{1}/$_2$ teaspoon onion powder

^{1}/$_2$ teaspoon ground red pepper

^{1}/$_2$ teaspoon ground cinnamon

Fresh parsley sprigs for garnish

◆ Place the pork tenderloins in a baking dish or sealable plastic bag. Combine the honey, soy sauce, water, brown sugar, ginger, garlic, ketchup, onion powder, red pepper and cinnamon in a bowl. Stir to mix well. Pour over the pork. Cover or seal and marinate in the refrigerator for 8 hours, turning the pork occasionally.

◆ Drain the pork, reserving the marinade. Grill the pork over medium-hot coals, turning often and basting with the reserved marinade, for 25 to 35 minutes or until a meat thermometer inserted in the thickest part registers 160 degrees. Discard any unused marinade. Slice the pork thinly and arrange on a serving platter. Garnish with parsley sprigs.

The hint of fresh ginger makes this pork tenderloin unique.

SERVES 10 TO 12

Couscous-Stuffed Portobello Mushrooms

6 to 8 portobello mushroom caps

1 cup balsamic vinegar and oil salad dressing

1 package flavored couscous (such as garlic or Parmesan)

1 cup finely chopped red bell pepper

1/4 cup thinly sliced green onions

1 1/2 cups chopped arugula or fresh spinach

1/2 cup shredded Parmesan cheese

4 ounces feta cheese, crumbled

Grated fresh Parmesan cheese to taste

◆ Combine the mushroom caps and salad dressing in a shallow bowl. Toss gently to coat. Let marinate for 1 hour.

◆ Prepare the couscous according to the package directions, adding the bell pepper when stirring in the seasoning. Remove from the heat and let stand for 5 minutes. Remove to a bowl and stir in the green onions, arugula, 1/2 cup Parmesan cheese and the feta cheese.

◆ Preheat the oven to 350 degrees.

◆ Arrange the mushroom caps close together in a 10×15-inch baking pan coated with nonstick cooking spray. Fill each cap with 1/2 to 1 cup of the couscous mixture, packing firmly. Sprinkle generously with Parmesan cheese.

◆ Bake for 15 to 20 minutes or until golden brown and bubbly.

A good-looking side dish, terrific with anything grilled. It can be prepared and chilled for up to twelve hours before baking.

SERVES 6 TO 8

Zesty Carrots

12 large carrots, peeled, quartered and cut into strips
1 cup light mayonnaise
1/2 cup water
1/4 cup prepared horseradish
Salt and pepper to taste
Bread crumbs

◆ Preheat the oven to 375 degrees.
◆ Cook the carrots in boiling water in a saucepan for 7 to 10 minutes or until tender. Drain and arrange the carrots in a greased 2-quart baking dish.
◆ Combine the mayonnaise, water and horseradish in a bowl. Season with salt and pepper. Stir to mix well. Pour over the carrots and sprinkle bread crumbs on top.
◆ Bake for 15 minutes.

Complements both pork and beef.

SERVES 8 TO 10

AT THE 2001 MASTERS® TOURNAMENT, TIGER WOODS WON HIS FOURTH CONSECUTIVE PROFESSIONAL MAJOR, AND IN 2002, HE BECAME ONLY THE THIRD PLAYER TO WIN CONSECUTIVE MASTERS® TITLES.

Marinated Garden Salad

1 pint grape tomatoes, halved
1 bunch green onions, chopped
2 ribs celery, diced
8 ounces white mushrooms, sliced
1/3 cup rice wine vinegar
2/3 cup olive oil

Salt and pepper to taste
2 heads leaf lettuce, torn
1 (11-ounce) can mandarin oranges,
   drained
4 ounces crumbled bleu cheese
Croutons

✦ Combine the tomatoes, green onions, celery and mushrooms in a sealable plastic bag. Add the vinegar and olive oil. Season with salt and pepper. Seal the bag and turn to mix. Let marinate for 3 to 4 hours.

✦ Combine the lettuce, vegetables with marinade, oranges, bleu cheese and croutons in a large salad bowl. Toss to coat.

Tossed salad meets marinated vegetables for a sweet-savory combination.

SERVES 8 TO 10

"I'LL BE HERE EVERY FIRST WEEK OF APRIL AND I WILL LOOK FORWARD TO THIS TOURNAMENT EVERY YEAR FOR THE REST OF MY LIFE."

—PHIL MICKELSON, 2004 MASTERS® CHAMPION

Lime Cake

1 (2-layer) package butter-recipe
    cake mix
2 tablespoons lime juice plus enough
    water to measure 1 cup
1/2 cup (1 stick) butter or margarine,
    softened
3 eggs

1 (14-ounce) can sweetened
    condensed milk
1/2 cup lime juice (4 or 5 limes)
1 cup heavy whipping cream,
    whipped, or 8 ounces whipped
    topping
Lime slices for garnish

◆ Combine the cake mix, lime juice with water, butter and eggs in a bowl. Stir until blended. Pour into 2 greased and floured 8-inch cake pans. Bake as directed on the cake mix package. Cool in the pans for 10 minutes. Remove to a wire rack to cool completely.

◆ Mix the sweetened condensed milk and 1/2 cup lime juice in a bowl. Fold in the whipped cream. Spread between the layers and over the top and side of the cake. Chill for 2 to 3 hours. Garnish with lime slices and serve.

An exquisite springtime cake.

SERVES 12

Picnicking at Georgia Golf Hall of Fame's Botanical Gardens, A Springtime Outing

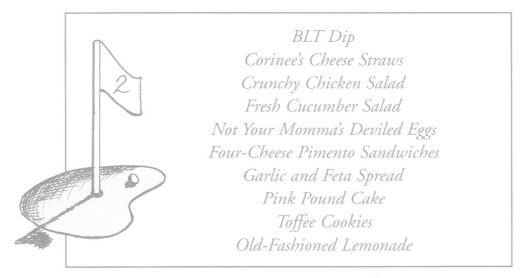

BLT Dip
Corinee's Cheese Straws
Crunchy Chicken Salad
Fresh Cucumber Salad
Not Your Momma's Deviled Eggs
Four-Cheese Pimento Sandwiches
Garlic and Feta Spread
Pink Pound Cake
Toffee Cookies
Old-Fashioned Lemonade

Augustans enjoy picnicking in the presence of some of the greatest golfers of all time at the Georgia Golf Hall of Fame's Botanical Gardens. Seven-foot-tall sculptures of Bobby Jones, Byron Nelson, Ben Hogan, Arnold Palmer, Raymond Floyd, and Jack Nicklaus all have permanent homes among the eight acres of beautiful display gardens.

Traditional picnic foods with a new twist are featured here. Enjoy serving favorites brightened with new flavors for your next on-the-go occasion!

Creating a picnic with pizzazz just takes a little creativity. Have fun with your packaging and presentation—using a variety of baskets adds a touch of warmth, along with versatility. Throw a colorful quilt on the ground for your tablecloth, and invert your largest basket to use as a table or serving spot. Divided baskets are helpful in transporting and then serving directly from the basket. Remember to use plenty of frozen ice packs or small resealable plastic bags filled with ice. For a special look, use a plastic-lined flower container, as we did, for serving the Crunchy Chicken Salad. Package and serve the Old-Fashioned Lemonade in individual canning jars.

Pound cakes with fruit are always popular for summer picnics in the South and may be cut into slices or small, bite-size wedges. Avoiding cakes with icing is recommended in the summer heat.

BLT Dip

1 pound bacon, crisp-cooked
   and crumbled
4 cups mayonnaise
1 cup sour cream

Chopped lettuce
1 pint grape tomatoes, quartered
Bagel chips or corn chips

◆ Mix the bacon, mayonnaise and sour cream in a bowl. Cover and chill overnight. Spread in the center of a serving platter. Surround with chopped lettuce and sprinkle with the tomatoes. Serve with bagel chips or corn chips.

SERVES 10

Corinee's Cheese Straws

1 pound sharp New York Cheddar
   cheese, shredded and softened
1/2 cup (1 stick) butter, softened
1 teaspoon baking powder

1/2 to 1 teaspoon cayenne pepper
1 teaspoon salt
1 1/2 cups all-purpose flour

◆ Preheat the oven to 325 degrees. Place the cheese and butter in a food processor fitted with a steel blade. Pulse until well mixed. Add the baking powder, cayenne pepper, salt and half the flour. Pulse to mix. Add the remaining flour and pulse until well mixed. Place the dough in a cookie press fitted with a star tip. Press onto a nonstick cookie sheet.
◆ Bake for 10 to 15 minutes or until the cheese straws have almost stopped sizzling. Remove to a wire rack to cool completely. Store in an airtight container.

This method delivers crisp, perfect cheese straws every time!

SERVES 10

Crunchy Chicken Salad

2 (3-ounce) packages chicken-flavor
   ramen noodles
3/4 cup vegetable oil
1/3 cup white vinegar
1/4 cup sugar
1 (12-ounce) package broccoli slaw
1 Red Delicious apple, cored
   and sliced

1 cup sunflower kernels
1 cup sweetened dried cranberries
   or raisins
1 bunch green onions, chopped
1 red bell pepper, chopped
1 cup slivered almonds
1 rotisserie chicken, boned
   and chopped

✦ Combine the contents of the seasoning packets from the ramen noodles, oil, vinegar and sugar in a bowl and mix well. Combine the broccoli slaw, apple, sunflower kernels, dried cranberries, green onions, bell pepper, almonds and chicken in a large bowl. Add the dressing and toss to coat.

✦ Crumble the ramen noodles and add just before serving. Toss to mix.

An unexpected combination of flavors and textures.

SERVES 8

BUILT ON WHAT WAS ONCE THE FRUITLAND NURSERIES, THE AUGUSTA NATIONAL COURSE IS HOME TO A WIDE VARIETY OF TREES, THE MOST COMMON OF WHICH IS THE LOBLOLLY PINE.

Fresh Cucumber Salad

3 cups sliced cucumbers
1/2 cup thinly sliced onion
1/2 teaspoon salt

1 cup sugar
1/2 cup white vinegar
1/2 teaspoon celery seeds

◆ Combine the cucumbers, onion and salt in a bowl. Toss to mix. Let stand for 1 hour.
◆ Combine the sugar, vinegar and celery seeds in a bowl. Stir to dissolve the sugar. Pour over the cucumber mixture. Cover and chill overnight.

Light and refreshing pickled cucumbers with minimal preparation.

SERVES 6 TO 8

Not Your Momma's Deviled Eggs

6 eggs
2 tablespoons finely chopped celery
1 green onion, finely chopped
2 ounces deli smoked ham, chopped

4 1/2 teaspoons capers, drained and
    finely chopped
1/4 cup light mayonnaise
1 tablespoon Dijon mustard

◆ Cover the eggs with water in a saucepan. Bring to a boil and cook for 15 minutes. Drain and cool immediately in ice water.
◆ Peel the eggs and cut in half lengthwise. Mash the egg yolks in a bowl. Add the celery, green onion, ham, capers, mayonnaise and Dijon mustard and mix well. Spoon into the egg whites. Cover and chill until ready to serve.

SERVES 12

Four-Cheese Pimento Sandwiches

3 cups (12 ounces) shredded white
    Cheddar cheese
2 cups (8 ounces) shredded yellow
    sharp Cheddar cheese
4 ounces crumbled bleu cheese
1 cup shredded Parmesan cheese

1 (4-ounce) jar sliced pimentos,
    drained
1 cup light mayonnaise
2 tablespoons Dijon mustard
Party-size loaf white bread or
    favorite bread, cut into slices

◆ Combine the white Cheddar cheese, yellow Cheddar cheese, bleu cheese, Parmesan cheese, pimentos, mayonnaise and Dijon mustard in a food processor and process until smooth. Remove to a bowl. Cover and chill.

◆ Spread on bread slices to make sandwiches.

Great as a sandwich spread or served as an appetizer with crackers and apple slices.

SERVES 12

Garlic and Feta Spread

2 teaspoons olive oil
2 tablespoons minced garlic
4 ounces feta cheese, crumbled

4 ounces cream cheese
Party rye bread

◆ Heat the olive oil in a skillet over low heat. Add the garlic and sauté until tender. Add the feta cheese and cream cheese and cook until the cheese melts, stirring constantly.

◆ Serve hot or cold as a spread for party rye bread or sprinkle with paprika and chopped parsley and serve with crackers or pita chips.

SERVES 12

Pink Pound Cake

3 cups all-purpose flour
1 teaspoon baking powder
1/2 teaspoon salt
4 eggs
1 cup milk
1 teaspoon vanilla extract

1 cup (2 sticks) margarine, softened
2 cups sugar
1 (3-ounce) box strawberry gelatin
1 (10-ounce) package frozen
    strawberries in syrup, thawed

◆ Preheat the oven to 325 degrees.

◆ Mix the flour, baking powder and salt together. Mix the eggs, milk and vanilla in a bowl. Beat the margarine, sugar and gelatin in a large bowl until light and fluffy. Stir in the dry ingredients alternately with the milk mixture. Fold in the strawberries. Pour into a nonstick bundt pan.

◆ Bake for 70 to 75 minutes or until a wooden pick inserted in the center comes out clean. Cool in the pan for 10 minutes. Remove to a wire rack to cool completely.

A pretty version of a Southern tradition.

SERVES 12

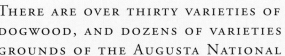

THERE ARE OVER THIRTY VARIETIES OF AZALEAS, SEVERAL STRAINS OF DOGWOOD, AND DOZENS OF VARIETIES OF ORNAMENTAL SHRUBS ON THE GROUNDS OF THE AUGUSTA NATIONAL GOLF CLUB.

Toffee Cookies

1/2 cup (1 stick) margarine, softened
1/2 cup shortening
1 cup packed light brown sugar
1/2 cup granulated sugar
2 eggs
2 teaspoons vanilla extract

2 1/2 cups all-purpose flour
1 teaspoon baking soda
1/2 teaspoon salt
1 (12-ounce) package miniature
   Heath bars, or 9 (1 1/2-ounce) Heath
   bars, crushed

✦ Preheat the oven to 375 degrees.
✦ Beat the margarine, shortening, brown sugar and granulated sugar in a large bowl until light and fluffy. Beat in the eggs and vanilla. Mix the flour, baking soda and salt together. Beat into the egg mixture. Fold in the crushed candy. Drop by teaspoonfuls onto an ungreased cookie sheet.
✦ Bake for 8 to 10 minutes. Let cool on the cookie sheet for 1 minute. Remove to a wire rack to cool completely.

—FROM *Second Round Tea-Time at the* MASTERS®

MAKES 4 DOZEN COOKIES

Old-Fashioned Lemonade

6 cups water
1 cup sugar

1/8 teaspoon salt
1/2 cup fresh lemon juice

✦ Combine the water, sugar and salt in a saucepan. Bring to a boil and boil for 2 minutes. Remove from the heat and chill for 1 hour.
✦ Pour into a 2-quart pitcher. Stir in the lemon juice. Serve over ice.

SERVES 6 TO 8

Cooking with Friends

Razmo
Tomato Poppers
Warm Goat Cheese Toasts
Grilled Beef Tenderloin Steaks
Grilled Pepper and Portobello Salad
Lemon Horseradish New Potatoes
Braised Brussels Sprouts with Pancetta
Caramel Walnut Pie with Port Wine Cherries

The invitation says to bring your own apron—this menu has all of the ingredients for a busy, active party!

The Cooking with Friends menu has been planned so that your guests get to know each other as they prepare the meal together. Choose this menu when you want to ensure that new neighbors leave your home as new friends, after collaborating in the kitchen.

Plan ahead of time which guests will be paired to prepare each dish, or leave it to chance and have guests draw a number to assign teams when they arrive. Decide which method will mix it up the best for your group.

Preparations for the hostess include providing work areas for each dish, complete with the recipe, ingredients, and utensils grouped together. Of course, at some point, someone will be asked to share the measuring spoons!

The stovetop, oven, and grill are all used, and the unique and quick appetizers are sure to inspire your guests as they work. Hosts may participate as chefs or may focus on keeping drinks refreshed and dishes rinsed. The pie can finish baking as the entrée is enjoyed.

Congratulations are sure to go around the table as everyone discusses their favorite flavors! This would be a fun occasion for giving special hostess awards for the best, worst, and messiest chefs, and for giving practical cooking-theme party favors.

Razmo

1 cup raspberry-flavored vodka

2 cups cranberry-raspberry
   juice cocktail

1/2 cup lime juice, sweetened

1/2 cup Triple Sec

Fresh raspberries for garnish

◆ Mix the vodka, cranberry-raspberry juice cocktail, lime juice and Triple Sec in a pitcher. Pour over ice in cocktail glasses. Garnish with fresh raspberries.

A raspberry Cosmopolitan.

SERVES 4

Tomato Poppers

1 pint grape tomatoes
Vodka

Kosher salt

◆ Place the tomatoes, vodka and salt in individual dipping bowls. Dip a tomato in vodka, then in salt and pop into your mouth.

A fun party conversation starter!

SERVES 10

"THAT'S WHAT THE MASTERS® IS ALL ABOUT TO ME—FRIENDS. IT'S A GREAT PRIVILEGE TO BE PART OF SUCH A WONDERFUL TRADITION SO MANY GREAT PEOPLE HAVE CONTRIBUTED TO. THE MEMORIES ALONE HAVE MADE ME A VERY HAPPY MAN."

—SAM SNEAD, THREE-TIME MASTERS® CHAMPION (1949, 1952, 1954)

Warm Goat Cheese Toasts

1 (8-ounce) thin baguette
4 ounces goat cheese, crumbled
1/4 cup honey

1/2 cup chopped walnuts or
  pecans, toasted
2 tablespoons chopped fresh rosemary

◆ Preheat the oven to 350 degrees. Slice the baguette on the diagonal into twenty 1/4-inch slices. Spread each with the cheese and arrange on a baking sheet. Bake for 10 minutes.
◆ Warm the honey in a saucepan over low heat. Stir in the walnuts. Remove the cheese toasts to a serving platter and top with the honey mixture. Sprinkle with the rosemary and serve.

Drizzled with honey and garnished with herbs, this hot hors d'oeuvre will vanish quickly.

SERVES 10

Grilled Beef Tenderloin Steaks

8 (1-inch) beef tenderloin steaks
Kosher salt
1/4 cup balsamic vinegar
2 tablespoons fresh lemon juice
1 cup red wine

1/4 cup coarsely chopped fresh
  rosemary
2 large garlic cloves, crushed
15 peppercorns
1/4 cup extra-virgin olive oil

◆ Arrange the steaks in a large glass baking dish. Rub salt gently into both sides of the meat.
◆ Whisk the vinegar, lemon juice, wine, rosemary, garlic and peppercorns in a bowl. Whisk in the olive oil gradually. Pour the marinade over the meat and turn to coat. Cover and marinate in the refrigerator for up to 12 hours, turning the meat several times.
◆ Remove the meat and discard the marinade. Cook the steaks on a hot grill to desired doneness.

This subtle marinade won't mask the true flavor of a quality cut of beef.

SERVES 8

Grilled Pepper and Portobello Salad

3/4 cup olive oil
2/3 cup balsamic vinegar
Salt and pepper to taste
1 1/2 pounds (about 6 large) portobello
  mushrooms, stems removed

3 large red bell peppers, halved
2 (5-ounce) packages spring mix
  salad greens

◆ Whisk the olive oil and vinegar in a bowl. Season with salt and pepper. Brush generously
on the mushrooms and peppers. Reserve the remaining dressing.
◆ Grill the mushrooms and peppers over medium heat for 6 minutes or until tender, turning
occasionally. Remove to a cutting board and let cool for 15 minutes.
◆ Cut the mushrooms and peppers into 1/2-inch wide strips and add to the reserved dressing.
Toss to coat.
◆ Line a serving platter with the salad greens. Top with the mushrooms and peppers and
drizzle with any remaining dressing.

Simple yet showy when presented on a large platter.

SERVES 8

EACH OF THE 18 HOLES AT THE AUGUSTA NATIONAL GOLF CLUB CARRIES
A BOTANICAL NAME—THE FIRST NINE BEGINS WITH TEA OLIVE AND ENDS
WITH CAROLINA CHERRY. THE SECOND NINE BEGINS WITH CAMELLIA AND
ENDS WITH THE PAR 4 HOLE NUMBER 18, HOLLY.

Lemon Horseradish New Potatoes

2 pounds new potatoes
1/4 cup (1/2 stick) butter
1/2 teaspoon salt
1/4 teaspoon pepper

2 teaspoons fresh lemon juice
4 1/2 teaspoons prepared horseradish
2 tablespoons chopped fresh parsley
   for garnish

◆ Preheat the oven to 350 degrees.
◆ Peel a 1/2-inch-wide strip around the center of each potato. Melt the butter in a 2-quart baking dish in the oven. Stir in the salt, pepper, lemon juice and horseradish. Add the potatoes and stir to coat. Cover with foil.
◆ Bake for 1 hour or until the potatoes are tender. Garnish with the parsley and drizzle with pan drippings when serving.

SERVES 8

"As I walked up to the 18th green, I distinctly remember thinking about the amount of emotion and drama the Masters® has on Sunday. The bank of spectators. The sun nearing the tips of those tall pines. The serenity and natural beauty of Augusta National. I thought of the nostalgia, the history, the unbelievable beauty of the course built on an old nursery. I thought of the special ways in which the club holds firm to its tradition. It was a little overwhelming. I was nervous. I could feel my heart pick up a few paces."

—MARK O'MEARA, MASTERS® CHAMPION (1998)

Braised Brussels Sprouts with Pancetta

1¹/2 cups fresh bread crumbs
2 teaspoons thyme
¹/4 cup olive oil
¹/4 cup (¹/2 stick) butter
2 tablespoons olive oil
2 pounds baby brussels sprouts,
   washed and trimmed or larger
   brussels sprouts, halved

Salt and pepper to taste
6 ounces diced pancetta
3 tablespoons minced shallots
1 tablespoon minced garlic
¹/2 cup balsamic vinegar
¹/2 cup chicken broth
2 tablespoons chopped fresh parsley

◆ Combine the bread crumbs, thyme and ¹/4 cup olive oil in a bowl. Toss to mix well. Spread on a baking sheet. Bake at 350 degrees for 10 to 12 minutes to toast. Remove to a bowl and set aside.

◆ Heat the butter and 2 tablespoons olive oil in a medium skillet. Add the brussels sprouts and season with salt and pepper. Cook until lightly browned, tossing often. Add the pancetta and sauté for 10 minutes or until well browned. Reduce the heat and add the shallots and garlic. Sauté for 2 minutes. Increase the heat to high and add the vinegar and broth. Cook for 10 minutes or until the brussels sprouts are glazed and tender, tossing often. Add more broth while cooking, if needed.

◆ Sprinkle with the toasted bread crumbs and parsley.

This recipe will change your mind about brussels sprouts.
It received rave reviews from our committee.

SERVES 8

Caramel Walnut Pie with Port Wine Cherries

1¹/4 cups dried tart cherries, chopped
¹/2 cup ruby port
²/3 cup packed brown sugar
²/3 cup light corn syrup
¹/4 cup (¹/2 stick) butter, melted
   and cooled to room temperature

3 eggs
1¹/2 teaspoons vanilla extract
1 cup walnuts, toasted and chopped
1 refrigerator pie pastry
Whipped cream or vanilla ice cream

◆ Preheat the oven to 350 degrees.

◆ Combine the cherries and wine in a heavy saucepan. Boil for 10 minutes or until the wine is absorbed, stirring often. Remove from the heat and let cool completely.

◆ Beat the brown sugar, corn syrup, melted butter and eggs in a large bowl with an electric mixer until foamy. Beat in the vanilla. Stir in the cherries and walnuts.

◆ Fit the pastry into a 9-inch pie plate. Pour the filling into the pie shell.

◆ Bake for 50 minutes or until the crust is golden brown and the center is just set. Remove to a wire rack to cool. Serve warm or at room temperature with whipped cream or ice cream.

Port-infused dried cherries add that extra dimension.

SERVES 8

Christening Celebration Luncheon

Red Delicious Cheese Spread
Green Jacket House Salad
Pesto Chicken Cheesecake
Tomato Pie
Carrot Soufflé
Spinach Squares
Sparkling Iced Tea
German's Sweet Chocolate Pies
or
Pink Lemonade Cake

Babies are a blessing, as is the opportunity to host a special family meal in honor of a child's christening day. Our family-friendly menu is perfect for the memorable gatherings that take place when welcoming a new baby, or for a graduation, promotion, or retirement celebration.

Have the Red Delicious Cheese Spread ready to pull from the refrigerator when you arrive home from the special ceremony. Your guests will appreciate the scrumptious Pesto Chicken Cheesecake, served with a selection of tasty vegetables and the legendary Green Jacket House Salad. The different textures offered by the Spinach Squares, Tomato Pie, and Carrot Soufflé make this variety of side dishes a treat to sample. And who wouldn't scramble for their slice of German's Sweet Chocolate Pie?

Decorations for a Christening Celebration Luncheon are a joy to assemble! Begin with pale pink or blue, accenting your table linens with sweet, lacy baby blankets. Use any silver rattles, cups, and baby spoons collected by the family. Add delicate ribbons to these precious accessories and arrange on the tables. Place nosegays in the silver baby cups for dainty table decorations. Pictures of the babies in the family, displayed in silver frames, are another thoughtful touch, sure to stir memories and conversation.

Red Delicious Cheese Spread

8 ounces cream cheese, chilled
4 1/2 teaspoons mayonnaise
1/4 cup sugar
1/2 cup chopped celery
1/2 cup chopped pecans

1 large Red Delicious apple, cored and
chopped
1 cup (4 ounces) shredded sharp
Cheddar cheese
Butter crackers

◆ Beat the cream cheese, mayonnaise and sugar in a bowl until light and fluffy. Add the celery, pecans, apple and cheese. Stir to mix well. Shape into a ball. Serve with butter crackers.

SERVES 10 TO 12

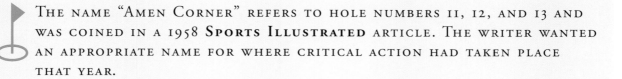

THE NAME "AMEN CORNER" REFERS TO HOLE NUMBERS 11, 12, AND 13 AND WAS COINED IN A 1958 **SPORTS ILLUSTRATED** ARTICLE. THE WRITER WANTED AN APPROPRIATE NAME FOR WHERE CRITICAL ACTION HAD TAKEN PLACE THAT YEAR.

Green Jacket House Salad

Pita bread for croutons
3 tablespoons vegetable oil
2 tablespoons red wine vinegar
1 teaspoon chopped fresh parsley
1 teaspoon seasoned salt
1 teaspoon dried oregano

1 bunch green onions, green part only, chopped
1 head iceberg lettuce, torn into bite-size pieces
1 tomato, diced
2 tablespoons grated Parmesan cheese

◆ Preheat the oven to 350 degrees. Cut the pita bread into small pieces and spread on a baking sheet. Bake for 5 to 7 minutes. Let cool and store in an airtight container.

◆ Whisk the oil, vinegar, parsley, seasoned salt, oregano and green onions in a bowl. Combine the pita croutons, lettuce, tomato and cheese in a large bowl. Add the dressing and toss to mix.

A green jacket is a prized possession of a Masters® Champion, owned only by Tournament winners and members of the Augusta National Golf Club. Named after the coveted award, The Green Jacket was for many years a popular local restaurant neighboring the Augusta National Golf Club. Their distinct house salad recipe has been widely circulated under many different names. We are bringing you the original.

Serves 6 to 8

Pesto Chicken Cheesecake

16 ounces cream cheese, softened
2 eggs
2 tablespoons all-purpose flour
3 tablespoons Pesto (below)

2 cups chopped cooked chicken
1 cup sour cream
1 tablespoon all-purpose flour
Basil leaves for garnish

◆ Preheat the oven to 325 degrees. Beat the cream cheese in a bowl with an electric mixer at medium speed until smooth. Add the eggs, 2 tablespoons flour and pesto and beat until blended. Stir in the chicken. Pour into a greased 8-inch springform pan. Bake for 30 minutes. Remove to a wire rack.

◆ Mix the sour cream and 1 tablespoon flour in a bowl. Spread evenly over the warm cheesecake. Bake at 325 degrees for 10 minutes. Remove to a wire rack. Loosen from the side of the pan with a sharp knife and remove the side. Serve hot or cold, garnished with basil leaves.

A mild basil flavor will appeal to a variety of palates. Simplify this recipe by substituting prepared pesto.

SERVES 6 TO 8

Pesto

1 1/2 cups firmly packed basil leaves
1/2 cup pecan pieces, toasted
1/2 cup olive oil

3 garlic cloves
3 tablespoons lemon juice
1/2 teaspoon salt

◆ Process the basil leaves, pecans, olive oil, garlic, lemon juice and salt in a food processor until smooth. Cover and chill any leftover pesto for up to 5 days or freeze.

MAKES ABOUT I CUP

Tomato Pie

2 tablespoons Dijon mustard
1 baked (9-inch) pie shell, cooled
6 to 8 Roma tomatoes, sliced
Salt and pepper to taste
2 tablespoons mayonnaise

1 cup (4 ounces) shredded white
   Cheddar cheese
1 cup (4 ounces) shredded yellow
   Cheddar cheese
3 tablespoons grated Parmesan cheese

◆ Preheat the oven to 350 degrees. Spread the Dijon mustard over the bottom of the baked pie shell. Arrange the sliced tomatoes in the pie shell and season with salt and pepper.
◆ Mix the mayonnaise, white Cheddar cheese and yellow Cheddar cheese in a bowl. Spread over the tomatoes. Sprinkle the Parmesan cheese on top. Bake for 20 minutes.

Roma tomatoes are an essential ingredient for a successful pie.

SERVES 8

Carrot Soufflé

1 1/4 pounds baby carrots
1/4 cup (1/2 stick) unsalted butter,
   melted
3/4 cup sugar

2 eggs, beaten
2 tablespoons self-rising flour
1 teaspoon vanilla extract

◆ Preheat the oven to 350 degrees.
◆ Cook the carrots in boiling water in a saucepan until tender. Drain and mash the carrots in a bowl. Add the melted butter, sugar, eggs, flour and vanilla and stir to mix well. Pour into a 2-quart baking dish. Bake for 30 to 40 minutes.

A sweet accompaniment.

SERVES 8

Spinach Squares

1/4 cup (1/2 stick) butter
3 eggs
1 cup all-purpose flour
1 teaspoon baking powder
1 teaspoon salt
1 cup milk

1 pound Monterey Jack cheese, shredded
1 sweet onion, grated
2 (10-ounce) packages frozen chopped spinach, thawed, drained and squeezed dry

◆ Preheat the oven to 350 degrees. Melt the butter in a 9×13-inch baking dish in the oven. Tilt to coat the dish evenly with melted butter.

◆ Beat the eggs in a bowl. Beat in the flour, baking powder, salt and milk. Add the cheese, onion and spinach and mix well. Pour into the prepared baking dish.

◆ Bake for 35 minutes or until a knife inserted in the center comes out clean. Cut into squares.

For a spicy variation, substitute Pepper Jack for Monterey Jack cheese.

SERVES 10 TO 12

Sparkling Iced Tea

4 cups boiling water
2 family-size tea bags
1 (12-ounce) can frozen lemonade
   concentrate, thawed
1/2 cup sugar

4 cups cold water
1 (1-liter) bottle ginger ale
Mint leaves, lemon and lime slices
   for garnish

◆ Pour 4 cups boiling water over the tea bags in a heatproof pitcher. Let steep for 15 minutes. Remove the tea bags and stir in the lemonade concentrate, sugar and 4 cups cold water. Cover and chill. Stir in the ginger ale just before serving.

◆ Pour over glasses filled with ice and garnish with mint leaves, lemon and lime slices.

Sweet tea is always a must at Southern occasions. Here is our fruity, fizzy version.

SERVES 12

German's Sweet Chocolate Pies

4 ounces German's sweet chocolate
1/4 cup (1/2 stick) butter
1 2/3 cups evaporated milk
1 1/2 cups sugar
3 tablespoons cornstarch
1/8 teaspoon salt

2 eggs
1 teaspoon vanilla extract
2 unbaked (9-inch) pie shells
1 1/3 cups flaked coconut
1/2 cup chopped pecans

◆ Preheat the oven to 375 degrees.
◆ Melt the chocolate and butter in a saucepan over low heat. Remove from the heat and stir in the evaporated milk gradually.
◆ Mix the sugar, cornstarch and salt in a bowl. Beat in the eggs and vanilla. Stir in the chocolate mixture gradually. Pour into the pie shells.
◆ Mix the coconut and pecans in a bowl. Sprinkle over the filling.
◆ Bake for 45 to 50 minutes. Remove to a wire rack and let cool for 4 hours before cutting.

These freeze great!

SERVES 16

THE MASTERS® IS GOLF'S YOUNGEST MAJOR TOURNAMENT, FIRST PLAYED IN 1934. THE BRITISH OPEN BEGAN IN 1860, THE U.S. OPEN IN 1895, AND THE PGA CHAMPIONSHIP IN 1916.

Pink Lemonade Cake

1 quart vanilla ice cream
1 (6-ounce) can frozen pink lemonade
  concentrate, thawed
5 to 6 drops red food coloring

1 (2-layer) package yellow cake mix
1 cup heavy whipping cream
2 tablespoons sugar

◆ Stir the ice cream in a bowl to soften. Stir in $1/3$ cup of the lemonade concentrate and the food coloring. Spread evenly in a foil-lined 9-inch cake pan. Freeze for 2 to 3 hours or until firm.

◆ Prepare the cake mix using the package directions. Pour the batter into 2 greased and floured 9-inch cake pans. Bake as directed on the cake mix package. Cool in the pans for 10 minutes. Remove to a wire rack to cool completely.

◆ Place 1 cake layer on a serving plate. Remove the frozen ice cream mixture from the cake pan and place on top of the cake layer. Top with the remaining cake layer.

◆ Beat the remaining lemonade concentrate, whipping cream and sugar in a bowl until stiff. Spread over the top and side of the cake. Freeze for at least 1 hour before serving.

SERVES 12

"Nach-O" Ordinary Birthday Party

Red Sangria
Little Jewels
Artichoke Salsa, Traditional Salsa, Avocado Salsa
Red and Chipotle Pepper Hummus
Baked Corn Dip
Mexican Bread Bowl
Mexican Pulled Pork Over Yellow Rice
Spinach Enchiladas with Sour Cream Sauce
Mexican Chopped Salad
or
Sugar Snap, Black Bean and Corn Sauté
Strawberry Margarita Pie

Guests will agree that this is "Not Your" Ordinary Birthday Party! Designed to celebrate a monumental birthday, whether it's thirty, forty, fifty, or beyond, this Mexican-themed menu is infused with flavor, color, and fun.

Santa Fe-style luminaries line the sidewalk, while the glow from candles and light strands dance off the colors of the table. Surprise your guests with the many varieties of colorful peppers available, grouped in small arrangements with avocados and fragrant cilantro.

Pewter, silver, and cobalt blue dishes blend refreshingly with terra cotta, stoneware, and traditional Mexican decorations such as maracas, piñatas, sombreros, and bright linens. Complete the setting by selecting mariachi music or hiring a guitarist.

Have a pitcher of Red Sangria ready to serve as guests arrive, and serve in fruit-garnished glasses. Little Jewels are martini-style margaritas served individually iced from the martini shaker.

Designed to satisfy a crowd, our appetizers supply plenty of flavor. Fresh ingredients add vivid colors and zest, while the variety of salsas invite everyone to choose their favorite.

Depending on the season, choose the crisp salad or the warm sauté. You'll find Mexican Pulled Pork Over Yellow Rice is a great do-ahead entrée. Strawberry Margarita Pie is the surprise ice cream dessert that's not your ordinary birthday cake!

Red Sangria

1/2 cup sugar
1 gallon red wine
1/2 cup Triple Sec
1/2 cup brandy
Juice of 6 lemons
Juice of 6 oranges

1 apple, cored and thinly sliced
1 orange, seeded and thinly sliced
3 cups club soda
Apple, orange and lemon slices
  for garnish

◆ Dissolve the sugar in the wine in a very large pitcher. Stir in the Triple Sec, brandy, lemon juice, orange juice, sliced apple and sliced orange. Cover and chill overnight. Stir in the club soda just before serving.

◆ Pour over glasses filled with ice and garnish with apple, orange and lemon slices.

If you're serving a crowd, use the Red Sangria recipe in the original
Tea-Time at the MASTERS®. It makes enough for twenty-five!

SERVES 16 TO 20

Little Jewels

1 ounce fresh lime juice
1 ounce Cointreau
2 ounces Jose Cuervo Gold tequila

Crushed ice
Lime wedges for garnish

◆ Combine the lime juice, Cointreau, tequila and ice in a martini shaker. Shake for 15 seconds or until thoroughly mixed.

◆ Pour into a chilled martini or margarita glass. Garnish with lime wedges.

A potent martini-style margarita.

SERVES 1

Artichoke Salsa

2 (14-ounce) cans Mexican-style
  stewed tomatoes
1 (8-ounce) can sliced mushrooms,
  drained
1 (14-ounce) can artichoke hearts,
  drained and quartered
1 (4-ounce) can chopped green chiles
  or jalapeño chiles

1 (4-ounce) can sliced black olives
1/2 cup red wine vinegar
1/4 cup chopped fresh cilantro, or
  2 tablespoons dried cilantro
1 teaspoon garlic salt
2 dashes of Tabasco sauce (optional)
Tortilla chips

◆ Coarsely chop the tomatoes, mushrooms and artichoke hearts with a food chopper or by hand. Place in a large bowl and toss to mix.

◆ Add the green chiles, olives, vinegar, cilantro and garlic salt and stir to mix. Add the Tabasco sauce and stir to mix. Serve with your favorite tortilla chips.

Try this spooned over chicken breasts fresh off the grill.

MAKES 5 CUPS

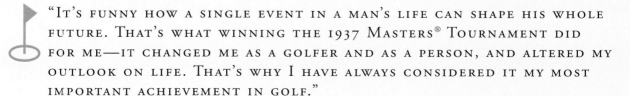

"IT'S FUNNY HOW A SINGLE EVENT IN A MAN'S LIFE CAN SHAPE HIS WHOLE FUTURE. THAT'S WHAT WINNING THE 1937 MASTERS® TOURNAMENT DID FOR ME—IT CHANGED ME AS A GOLFER AND AS A PERSON, AND ALTERED MY OUTLOOK ON LIFE. THAT'S WHY I HAVE ALWAYS CONSIDERED IT MY MOST IMPORTANT ACHIEVEMENT IN GOLF."

—BYRON NELSON, TWO-TIME MASTERS® CHAMPION (1937, 1942)

Traditional Salsa

1 (10-ounce) can tomatoes with green chiles
1 large tomato, seeded and chopped
2 green onions, chopped
1 garlic clove, minced

Juice of $1/2$ lime
1 tablespoon chopped fresh cilantro
$1/2$ teaspoon salt
Cumin and chili powder to taste
Tortilla chips

◆ Combine the tomatoes with green chiles, tomato, green onions, garlic, lime juice, cilantro and salt in a bowl. Season with cumin and chili powder. Stir to mix well. Serve with tortilla chips.

Your standard for any Mexican dinner.

MAKES 2 CUPS

Avocado Salsa

6 Roma tomatoes, seeded and chopped
3 firm avocados, chopped
4 green onions, chopped
1 (4-ounce) can chopped green chiles
3 tablespoons vegetable oil

1 to 2 garlic cloves, minced
Juice of 1 lime
$1 1/2$ teaspoons apple cider vinegar
Salt and pepper to taste
Tortilla chips

◆ Combine the tomatoes, avocados, green onions and green chiles in a bowl. Whisk the oil, garlic, lime juice and vinegar in a small bowl. Season with salt and pepper.
◆ Pour the vinegar mixture over the vegetables and toss gently to mix. Cover and chill for at least 1 hour. Serve with tortilla chips.

As delicious as it is colorful.

MAKES 5 CUPS

Red and Chipotle Pepper Hummus

1 red bell pepper, roasted, peeled and seeded, or prepared roasted red pepper

2 chipotle chiles in adobo sauce

1 (15-ounce) can garbanzo beans, drained and rinsed

1 garlic clove, minced

3 tablespoons tahini (sesame seed paste)

2 tablespoons lemon juice

2 tablespoons olive oil

2 tablespoons chopped fresh parsley

2 tablespoons soy sauce

$1^1/2$ teaspoons cumin

$1/8$ teaspoon salt

$1/2$ teaspoon cayenne pepper (optional)

Pita chips or lime-flavored tortilla chips

◆ Combine the roasted bell pepper, chipotle chiles in adobo sauce, garbanzo beans, garlic, tahini, lemon juice, olive oil, parsley, soy sauce, cumin, salt and cayenne pepper in a food processor or blender. Process until smooth.

◆ Remove to a bowl and serve with pita chips or lime-flavored tortilla chips.

To roast peppers, place them directly on a gas flame or under a broiler and roast until charred on all sides. Place them in a paper bag and let stand for 10 minutes; the skins will slip off easily.

MAKES 2 CUPS

Baked Corn Dip

3 (11-ounce) cans Mexicorn, drained
3 cups (12 ounces) shredded
  mozzarella cheese
1/2 cup grated fresh Parmesan cheese
3 cups mayonnaise

1 1/2 teaspoons chopped jalapeño
  chiles
Dash of salt
Corn chips

◆ Preheat the oven to 350 degrees. Combine the Mexicorn, mozzarella cheese, Parmesan cheese, mayonnaise, jalapeño chiles and salt in a bowl. Stir to mix well.
◆ Spoon into a 9×13-inch baking dish. Bake for 30 minutes. Serve hot with corn chips.

SERVES 18 TO 20

Mexican Bread Bowl

8 ounces cream cheese, softened
2 cups sour cream
1 (2-ounce) jar dried beef, minced
2 cups (8 ounces) shredded sharp
  Cheddar cheese
1 (4-ounce) can chopped green chiles

1 (2-ounce) jar pimentos, drained and
  chopped
1 bunch green onions, chopped
Dash of Worcestershire sauce
1 round loaf sourdough bread
Corn chips

◆ Preheat the oven to 350 degrees.
◆ Combine the cream cheese, sour cream, dried beef, Cheddar cheese, drained green chiles, pimentos, green onions and Worcestershire sauce in a large bowl. Stir to mix well.
◆ Cut the top off the bread and hollow out the inside to make room for the dip. Fill the cavity with the cheese mixture and replace the top on the bread. Wrap the loaf in foil and place on a baking sheet. Bake for 1 to 1 1/2 hours. Remove the top and serve with corn chips.

SERVES 10 TO 12

Mexican Pulled Pork Over Yellow Rice

1 onion, chopped
1 (3^1/$_2$-pound) boneless pork
   shoulder roast
1 (14^1/$_2$-ounce) can diced tomatoes
   with jalapeño chiles
1 (4-ounce) can chopped green chiles
1 (11-ounce) can yellow whole kernel
   corn, drained
1 teaspoon garlic powder

1 teaspoon salt
2 teaspoons cumin
1^1/$_2$ teaspoons dried oregano
^{1}/$_2$ teaspoon cayenne pepper
3 tablespoons tomato paste
1 (16-ounce) package yellow
   saffron rice
Sour cream and chopped fresh cilantro
   for garnish

◆ Combine the onion and pork roast in a slow cooker.

◆ Mix the tomatoes with jalapeño chiles, green chiles, corn, garlic powder, salt, cumin, oregano and cayenne pepper in a bowl. Pour over the roast. Cover and cook on High for 5 hours or until cooked through and very tender.

◆ Remove the roast to a work surface and shred with a fork. Remove 1^1/$_2$ cups of liquid from the slow cooker and discard. Add the tomato paste to the slow cooker and stir to mix well. Cover and cook on High for 30 minutes. Return the shredded meat to the slow cooker and heat through.

◆ Cook the rice according to the package directions. Serve the pork mixture over the rice and garnish with sour cream and chopped cilantro.

A Southern favorite with a Southwestern flair.

SERVES 12

Spinach Enchiladas with Sour Cream Sauce

1 tablespoon unsalted butter
6 ounces fresh mushrooms,
   thinly sliced
Salt and freshly ground pepper
   to taste
1 large zucchini, coarsely chopped
1 (10-ounce) package frozen chopped
   spinach, thawed, drained and
   squeezed dry
1 tablespoon extra-virgin olive oil
1 tablespoon unsalted butter
1 onion, finely chopped
1 garlic clove, pressed

2 jalapeño chiles, seeded and finely
   chopped
1 teaspoon dried oregano
1 (4-ounce) can black olives, drained
   and finely chopped
1/2 cup crumbled cotija cheese or feta
   cheese
3/4 cup (3 ounces) shredded
   mozzarella cheese
1 package (8-inch) flour tortillas
1/4 cup (1/2 stick) unsalted butter,
   melted
Sour Cream Sauce (page 57)

◆ Melt 1 tablespoon butter in a large skillet over medium-high heat. Add the mushrooms and season with salt and pepper. Sauté until the mushrooms begin to brown. Remove from the heat and set aside. Pulse the zucchini in a food processor to coarsely chop. Add the spinach and pulse to chop. Heat the olive oil and 1 tablespoon butter in a large saucepan over medium heat. Add the onion, garlic, jalapeño chiles and oregano. Sauté for 8 minutes or until the onion is tender but not browned. Add the spinach mixture and olives and sauté for 5 minutes or until the mixture is hot and the liquid has evaporated. Season with salt. Remove from the heat and let cool for 5 minutes. Stir in the cotija cheese and mozzarella cheese.

◆ Lay the tortillas on a work surface. Spoon the spinach mixture on the tortillas and top with the mushrooms. Roll up the tortillas and arrange in a baking dish. Brush with the melted butter. Top with Sour Cream Sauce. Bake at 350 degrees for 15 minutes or until hot and bubbly.

A distinctive choice for a vegetarian entrée.

Serves 6

Sour Cream Sauce

¹/₂ cup (1 stick) butter
¹/₂ cup all-purpose flour
2 cups hot chicken broth

1 cup sour cream
1 (4-ounce) can chopped green chiles

◆ Melt the butter in a saucepan. Remove from the heat and stir in the flour. Return to the heat and whisk for a few minutes. Remove from the heat and whisk in the broth.
◆ Whisk in the sour cream. Return to the heat and cook until thickened, stirring constantly. Thin with additional broth if the sauce seems too thick. Stir in the green chiles.

This sauce can be made ahead and reheated when ready to assemble the enchiladas (page 56).

MAKES 3 CUPS

"WHEN YOU GO TO THE CHAMPIONS' DINNER AND LOOK AROUND AT EVERYONE IN THEIR GREEN COATS, YOU REALIZE YOU'RE A MEMBER OF ONE OF THE MOST EXCLUSIVE GROUPS OF PEOPLE IN THE WORLD."

—SAM SNEAD, THREE-TIME MASTERS® CHAMPION (1949, 1952, 1954) AND RECIPIENT OF THE FIRST MASTERS® COAT IN 1949

Mexican Chopped Salad

1 large seedless cucumber, cut into
    bite-size pieces
4 tomatoes, seeded and cut into
    bite-size pieces
6 ribs celery hearts with leaves, cut
    into bite-size pieces
1 green bell pepper, diced

1 red onion, diced
1/3 cup chopped fresh cilantro
1/2 cup canola oil
1/4 cup red wine vinegar
Juice of 2 limes
Salt and pepper to taste

◆ Combine the cucumber, tomatoes, celery, bell pepper, onion and cilantro in a large bowl.
◆ Whisk the oil, vinegar and lime juice in a bowl. Season with salt and pepper. Pour over the vegetables and toss to coat. Cover and chill for at least 3 hours to blend the flavors.

SERVES 10 TO 12

Sugar Snap, Black Bean and Corn Sauté

Vegetable oil
2 pounds sugar snap peas, strings
    removed
1 (16-ounce) can black beans, drained

1 (16-ounce) bag frozen corn
1 red onion, finely chopped
Cumin to taste

◆ Heat a small amount of oil in a large skillet. Add the snap peas, black beans, corn and onion. Sauté until the vegetables are tender. Season with cumin.

*Reduce the snap peas to one pound for a quick and easy
side dish for any family Mexican meal.*

SERVES 12

Strawberry Margarita Pie

1 1/4 cups crushed pretzels
1/4 cup sugar
1/2 cup (1 stick) margarine, melted
1 (14-ounce) can sweetened
   condensed milk
1/2 cup frozen margarita mix
   concentrate, thawed

1 (10-ounce) package frozen
   strawberries in syrup, thawed
8 ounces whipped topping, or 2 cups
   heavy whipping cream, whipped

◆ Mix the pretzels, sugar and melted margarine in a bowl. Press firmly onto the bottom of an ungreased 8- or 9-inch springform pan; chill.

◆ Combine the sweetened condensed milk and margarita mix in a large bowl. Beat with an electric mixer until smooth. Add the strawberries and beat at low speed until mixed. Fold in the whipped topping. Pour into the prepared crust. Cover and freeze for at least 3 hours or overnight.

◆ Let stand at room temperature for 30 minutes before serving.

SERVES 10

AUGUSTA NATIONAL'S OFFICIAL OPENING TOOK PLACE IN JANUARY OF 1933, WHEN A PRIVATE TRAIN BROUGHT MEMBERS AND PROSPECTIVE MEMBERS FROM NEW YORK CITY TO AUGUSTA FOR A WEEKEND OF GOLF. FOR ONE HUNDRED DOLLARS, THE "TRAIN PARTY" GUESTS RECEIVED A PULLMAN BERTH, A ROOM AT THE BON AIR, ALL MEALS AND TRANSPORTATION, AND THREE DAYS OF GOLF WITH BOBBY JONES.

Cruising on the Augusta Canal,
A Sunset Supper

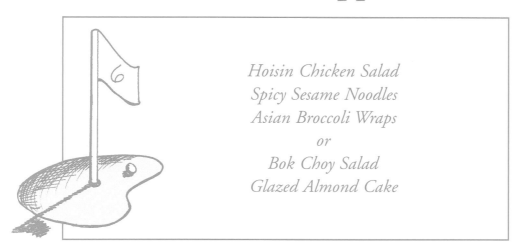

Hoisin Chicken Salad
Spicy Sesame Noodles
Asian Broccoli Wraps
or
Bok Choy Salad
Glazed Almond Cake

Bobby Jones and Clifford Roberts went to great effort to build an international field from the beginning of the Masters® Tournament. Bobby Jones himself was a three-time champion of the British Open and a British Amateur Champion. Gary Player became the first international Masters® Champion in 1961, and the native South African won again in 1974 and 1978. Spaniard Seve Ballesteros became the first Masters® Champion from Europe in 1980 and led the field again in 1983. Since then, other champions from England, Wales, Scotland, Germany, Spain, Canada, and Fiji have helped to build Masters® history.

The international contribution to the construction of the city of Augusta was also significant. The roots of Augusta's Chinese community can be traced to the 1870s, when several hundred Chinese workers arrived to assist in the expansion of the Augusta Canal. The Chinese men had completed work on the transcontinental railroad, and worked alongside Italian stonemasons and Irish laborers to enlarge the canal to three times its original size. The Augusta Canal fueled the industrial revolution of Augusta—textile mills used the energy from flowing water for their machines. During this expansion, the famous Rae's Creek, which still provides a water hazard to the Masters® competitors of today, was dammed to create Lake Olmstead.

The Augusta Canal National Heritage Area, one of only eighteen National Heritage Areas designated by Congress, is a valuable natural and recreational resource for the region. Our chilled Asian-style supper would be a popular choice to take on a boat cruise, or to savor after a stroll along the canal trail, with its beautiful views of wildlife and the Savannah River.

Hoisin Chicken Salad

2¹/2 to 3 pounds bone-in chicken
  breasts
Olive oil
Salt and pepper to taste
2 ribs celery, diced
3 green onions, chopped
2 tablespoons chopped fresh cilantro
  or parsley

¹/3 cup rice wine vinegar
3 tablespoons hoisin sauce
1 tablespoon minced fresh ginger
4¹/2 teaspoons soy sauce
3 tablespoons canola oil
1 tablespoon sesame oil

◆ Arrange the chicken in a foil-lined roasting pan. Brush with olive oil and season with salt and pepper. Bake at 375 degrees for 40 minutes or until cooked through. Remove the chicken to a work surface and let cool. Shred the chicken into bite-size pieces, discarding the skin and bones. Combine the chicken, celery, green onions and cilantro in a large bowl.
◆ Whisk the vinegar, hoisin sauce, ginger and soy sauce in a small bowl. Whisk in the canola oil and sesame oil slowly. Pour over the chicken mixture and toss to coat. Cover and chill.

An Asian-infused "no-mayo" chicken salad.

SERVES 6 TO 8

ONE OF THE FIRST WISTERIA VINES TO BE ESTABLISHED IN THE U.S. CAN BE SEEN ADJACENT TO THE CLUBHOUSE AT AUGUSTA NATIONAL. IT IS ALSO BELIEVED TO BE THE LARGEST VINE OF ITS KIND IN THE COUNTRY.

Spicy Sesame Noodles

3 scallions
12 ounces soba noodles or linguini
3 tablespoons rice wine vinegar
1 tablespoon tahini (sesame seed
    paste)
2 tablespoons peanut butter
1 tablespoon honey mustard
2 tablespoons soy sauce

$1/3$ cup sesame oil
1 tablespoon chile oil
$1/3$ cup freshly squeezed orange juice
Salt and pepper to taste
2 tablespoons toasted sesame seeds
1 carrot, grated
Sliced scallions and toasted sesame
    seeds for garnish

◆ Cut the scallions into $2^1/2$-inch pieces. Sliver the ends to make brushes. Place the scallion brushes in a bowl of ice water and set aside.

◆ Cook the noodles according to the package directions. Drain, rinse with cold water and let drain thoroughly.

◆ Whisk the vinegar, tahini, peanut butter, honey mustard and soy sauce in a large bowl. Mix the sesame oil and chile oil in a small bowl. Whisk slowly into the peanut butter mixture. Whisk in the orange juice. Season with salt and pepper. Drain the scallions. Add the scallions, noodles, sesame seeds and grated carrot. Toss to coat. Cover and chill for at least 1 hour. Garnish each serving with sliced scallions and sesame seeds.

SERVES 8

Asian Broccoli Wraps

1 (10-ounce) package broccoli slaw
1 (8-ounce) can water chestnuts,
   drained and slivered
1/2 cup chopped green onions

3 tablespoons sesame oil
6 tablespoons plum sauce
6 burrito-size flour tortillas

◆ Combine the broccoli slaw, water chestnuts and green onions in a bowl. Whisk the sesame oil and plum sauce in a small bowl. Add to the vegetables and toss to coat. Lay the tortillas on a work surface. Spoon the broccoli mixture onto the tortillas. Fold over and roll up the tortillas.

For transporting to a picnic, roll the wraps individually in plastic wrap.

SERVES 6

Bok Choy Salad

1/2 cup red wine vinegar
1/2 cup sugar
1 tablespoon soy sauce
1/2 cup olive oil
1/4 cup (1/2 stick) margarine

2 (3-ounce) packages ramen noodles
1/4 cup slivered almonds
1/4 cup sesame seeds
1 head bok choy, chopped
3 green onions, chopped

◆ Whisk the vinegar, sugar and soy sauce in a small bowl. Whisk in the olive oil slowly and set aside. Melt the margarine in a skillet. Crush the ramen noodles in the package. Discard the seasoning packets. Sauté the crushed noodles, almonds and sesame seeds until golden brown; drain on paper towels. Combine the bok choy and green onions in a large bowl. Add the noodle mixture and dressing. Toss to mix and serve immediately.

This vivid salad pairs well with any simply grilled meat or chicken.

SERVES 6 TO 8

Glazed Almond Cake

Cake

2 1/2 cups all-purpose flour
2 teaspoons baking powder
1/2 teaspoon salt
1/2 cup ground almonds
1 cup (2 sticks) butter, softened
2 cups sugar
4 eggs
1 1/2 teaspoons vanilla extract
1 1/2 teaspoons almond extract
1 cup milk

Glaze

1/4 cup milk
3/4 cup sugar
1/2 teaspoon almond extract
1/2 cup sliced almonds, toasted

◆ *For the cake,* preheat the oven to 350 degrees.

◆ Mix the flour, baking powder, salt and ground almonds together. Beat the butter and sugar in a bowl until light and fluffy. Add the eggs 1 at a time, beating well after each addition. Beat in the vanilla extract and almond extract. Beat in the dry ingredients alternately with the milk; do not overmix. Pour into a greased and floured 10-inch bundt pan.

◆ Bake for 60 to 70 minutes or until a wooden pick inserted in the center comes out clean. Cool in the pan for 10 minutes. Invert onto a wire rack and cool for 10 minutes.

◆ *For the glaze,* beat the milk, sugar, almond extract and sliced almonds in a bowl until well mixed.

◆ Slide a piece of waxed paper under the rack. Pour the glaze over the warm cake.

SERVES 12

Summer Supper Club

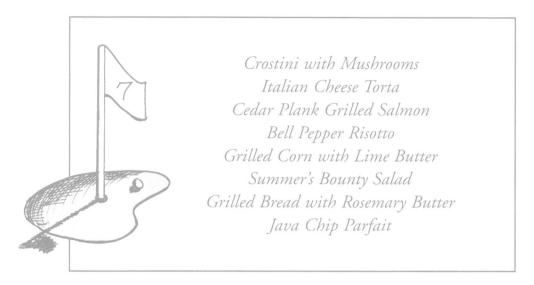

Crostini with Mushrooms
Italian Cheese Torta
Cedar Plank Grilled Salmon
Bell Pepper Risotto
Grilled Corn with Lime Butter
Summer's Bounty Salad
Grilled Bread with Rosemary Butter
Java Chip Parfait

When you belong to a Supper Club, the venues, meals, and even the crowd can change from gathering to gathering. While different Supper Clubs have different guidelines, one rule is a constant: you are bound to have a blast!

Food cooked on the grill is a ritual in Augusta, so these recipes are perfect for hosting Supper Club during the warmer months. Celebrating simplicity and freshness, this particular menu takes advantage of summer's flavorful bounty and a fun new grilling technique.

Your group may decide to keep a food journal, placing pictures and menus from each evening in a scrapbook, where guests write their comments and reflections.

Creative place cards will stir up conversation—choose adjectives to define each guest and have everyone try to find their seat at the table!

Entertaining can be one of life's great pleasures—setting the table, pulling out all of your pretties, lighting the candles—*or not*. You can make it as simple or as elegant as you please, as long as it is a style with which you are comfortable. After all, the most important thing is reveling in laughs and good food with friends.

Crostini with Mushrooms

3 tablespoons butter
7 ounces shiitake mushrooms, stems
  removed, caps coarsely chopped
4 ounces cremini mushrooms,
  coarsely chopped
2 garlic cloves, minced
1/2 cup heavy cream
1/4 to 1/2 cup crumbled bleu cheese

1/2 cup (about 2 1/2 ounces) thinly
  sliced proscuitto, chopped
Salt and pepper to taste
18 (1/2-inch) diagonally cut
  sourdough baguette slices
Olive oil
Chopped fresh parsley

◆ Melt the butter in a large heavy skillet over medium-high heat. Add the shiitake mushrooms, cremini mushrooms and garlic. Sauté for 10 minutes or until the mushrooms are tender and browned. Add the cream and cook until all the liquid is absorbed. Remove from the heat. Add the bleu cheese and stir until the cheese melts. Stir in the proscuitto. Season with salt and pepper.

◆ Preheat the oven to 375 degrees.

◆ Arrange the baguette slices on a baking sheet. Brush with olive oil. Bake for 5 minutes or until golden brown. Top each bread slice with 1 generous tablespoonful of the mushroom mixture. Bake for 6 minutes or until heated through. Sprinkle with chopped parsley.

The mushroom topping can be made one day ahead.
Cover and chill until needed.

SERVES 18

Italian Cheese Torta

1 cup (2 sticks) margarine, chilled and cut into pieces
12 ounces feta cheese, crumbled
8 ounces cream cheese, softened
2 garlic cloves, chopped
1 shallot, chopped

$1/2$ cup white wine
$1/2$ cup pine nuts, lightly toasted
1 cup sun-dried tomatoes packed in oil, drained and chopped
1 cup prepared pesto
Water crackers

◆ Process the margarine, feta cheese, cream cheese, garlic, shallot and wine in a food processor until well mixed.
◆ Line a 5×9-inch loaf pan with plastic wrap and coat with nonstick cooking spray. Sprinkle half the pine nuts in the bottom of the pan. Sprinkle half the tomatoes over the nuts. Spread half the pesto over the tomatoes. Spread with half the cheese mixture. Repeat the layers.
◆ Fold the plastic wrap over the top to seal. Chill overnight. Invert onto a serving plate and serve with water crackers.

Great for a large cocktail party, or divide in half for a smaller gathering, using a 4×8-inch loaf pan.

SERVES 25

FROM THE AGE OF NINE, WHEN HE STARTED PLAYING GOLF AT THE AUGUSTA COUNTRY CLUB, JUST OVER THE FENCE FROM AUGUSTA NATIONAL, 1987 MASTERS® CHAMPION LARRY MIZE KNEW HE WANTED TO BE A PROFESSIONAL GOLFER.

Cedar Plank Grilled Salmon

1 tablespoon paprika
1 tablespoon kosher salt
2 teaspoons brown sugar
2 teaspoons lemon pepper
1 teaspoon granulated garlic
1 teaspoon dried tarragon

1 teaspoon dried basil
6 to 8 (6- to 8-ounce) 2-inch-thick
   salmon fillets, skin removed
Lemon juice
Lemon wedges for garnish

◆ Soak cedar grilling planks in water for at least 4 hours or overnight.
◆ Process the paprika, salt, brown sugar, lemon pepper, garlic, tarragon and basil in a small food processor.
◆ Place the salmon on waxed paper. Sprinkle each fillet with about 1 1/2 teaspoons of the seasoning mix, rubbing it into all sides of the salmon. Store any leftover seasoning in an airtight container. Remove the fillets to a platter and refrigerate, uncovered, for 2 to 12 hours.
◆ Arrange the salmon on the drained grilling planks. Squeeze lemon juice over the fillets. Place the planks on a preheated grill. Cover the grill and cook over medium heat for 10 minutes or until the fish flakes easily.
◆ Some crackling and smoke is normal, but spray the plank with water if it begins to flame. Serve the salmon garnished with additional lemon wedges.

A wonderful smoky flavor and fun to prepare. Find grilling planks
in the seafood section of your grocer or at specialty food stores.

SERVES 6 TO 8

Bell Pepper Risotto

3 cups chicken stock

1 tablespoon olive oil

1 large onion, chopped

1 large red bell pepper, diced

1 orange bell pepper, diced

2 garlic cloves, minced

1 cup arborio rice

1/2 cup freshly grated Parmesan cheese

Salt and pepper to taste

◆ Pour the stock into a small saucepan. Keep warm over low heat.

◆ Heat the olive oil in a large saucepan over medium-high heat. Add the onion and sauté for 3 to 4 minutes. Add the red bell pepper, orange bell pepper and garlic and sauté for 3 to 4 minutes. Add the rice and sauté for 1 minute. Add 1 ladleful of stock and stir to mix. Adjust heat to simmer.

◆ Continue adding stock, 1 ladleful at a time. Cook until the stock is absorbed before adding more, stirring frequently. Cook for a total time of 20 to 25 minutes or until the rice is tender. Stir in the cheese and season with salt and pepper.

SERVES 6 TO 8

Grilled Corn with Lime Butter

1/4 cup (1/2 stick) butter, melted
Juice of 2 limes
1 teaspoon salt

1/2 teaspoon pepper
1 dozen ears Silver Queen corn,
   husked

◆ Mix the butter, lime juice, salt and pepper in a shallow dish. Roll the ears of corn in the butter mixture or brush it on the corn.

◆ Grill the corn over a hot fire for 5 to 10 minutes or until lightly browned on all sides, turning occasionally. Remove to a platter and let cool to room temperature before serving.

Lime is the secret ingredient that makes this corn on the cob everyone's favorite.

SERVES 12

Summer's Bounty Salad

2 large seedless cucumbers
1/3 cup red wine vinegar
1 tablespoon sugar
1 teaspoon salt
2/3 cup coarsely chopped Vidalia
   onion or other sweet onion

3 large tomatoes, chopped
1/2 cup chopped fresh mint
3 tablespoons olive oil
8 ounces mozzarella cheese, cubed
Salt and pepper to taste

◆ Slice the cucumbers in half lengthwise. Cut on the diagonal into 1/2-inch slices. Mix the cucumbers, vinegar, sugar and salt in a large bowl. Let stand for 1 hour, stirring occasionally. Add the onion, tomatoes, mint, olive oil and cheese. Season with salt and pepper. Toss to mix.

The best of your summer garden accented with mint.

SERVES 10

Grilled Bread with Rosemary Butter

2 tablespoons butter, softened
2 tablespoons chopped fresh rosemary
6 tablespoons extra-virgin olive oil
1 cup grated Parmesan cheese
5 garlic cloves, minced
1 baguette

◆ Process the butter and rosemary in a food processor until mixed. Add the olive oil gradually, processing until well mixed. Add the cheese and garlic and process until well mixed.
◆ Cut the bread in half lengthwise. Slice each half diagonally at 1^1/2-inch intervals, cutting ^{3}/4 of the way through the bread. Spread the butter mixture between the slices and on top of the bread.
◆ Wrap the bread in foil and grill for 8 minutes, or place unwrapped, cut side up, on a baking sheet and bake at 400 degrees for 8 to 10 minutes or until the edges are crisp.

SERVES 6 TO 8

Java Chip Parfait

2 (3-ounce) scoops Java Chip coffee
ice cream
2 to 3 teaspoons Tia Maria liqueur
1 tablespoon flaked coconut, toasted

◆ Place the ice cream in decorative glasses or a bowl. Drizzle the liqueur over the ice cream and sprinkle with the coconut. Serve immediately.

A luscious blend of chocolate chunks and coffee ice cream.

SERVES 1

Engagement Cocktail Party

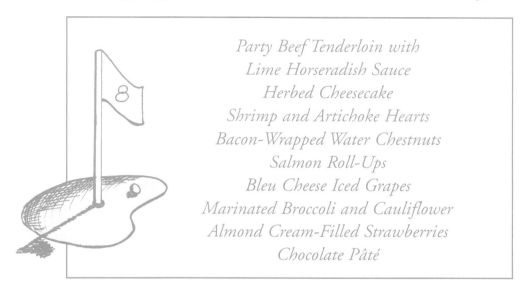

Party Beef Tenderloin with
Lime Horseradish Sauce
Herbed Cheesecake
Shrimp and Artichoke Hearts
Bacon-Wrapped Water Chestnuts
Salmon Roll-Ups
Bleu Cheese Iced Grapes
Marinated Broccoli and Cauliflower
Almond Cream-Filled Strawberries
Chocolate Pâté

Kick off the wedding season for a newly engaged couple, announcing and celebrating the upcoming marriage with the families and friends of the bride and groom. Setting the scene for comfortable introductions for the couple's parents and their friends, as well as the close friends of the engaged couple, a cocktail party is perfect for this occasion, allowing everyone to mingle with ease.

An elegant meal featuring all finger foods has been designed for you—no utensils are necessary to savor this variety of superb hors d'oeuvres while standing and moving to wherever the conversation takes you.

In Augusta, Georgia, it is customary for several couples to host an engagement party, and, traditionally, they are friends of the bride's or groom's parents. A cooperative effort among hostesses allows for a wide selection of cuisine that may be arranged as a bountiful buffet or as small tasting stations.

This grand offering of cocktail foods includes a classic beef tenderloin and standout shrimp and salmon choices that are substantial enough to leave your guests feeling satisfied. Bleu Cheese Iced Grapes are a sweet, juicy surprise with the added complexity of bleu cheese. Almond Cream-Filled Strawberries and the arrangement of Chocolate Pâté provide visual treats, as well as delightful tastes that will be at least one of the topics of conversation!

Hiring a bartender for cocktail parties frees the hosts to focus on the fun of socializing. Having more than one bar set up is wise to accommodate the flow of guests through the room.

The circumstances of the couple dictate so much—an Engagement Cocktail Party can be quite a large event, even if a smaller guest list is planned for the wedding or if the wedding will be held at a distant locale. Everyone will want a chance to share in the celebration with the engaged couple!

Party Beef Tenderloin

1 (6-pound) beef tenderloin, trimmed
1 garlic clove, halved
1/2 cup dry red wine
3 tablespoons low-sodium soy sauce
1/2 teaspoon hot sauce
1 teaspoon dried thyme

1/2 teaspoon pepper
1/4 teaspoon salt
1 bay leaf
Small rolls
Lime Horseradish Sauce (below)

✦ Prick the beef tenderloin with a fork and rub with the garlic. Combine the garlic, wine, soy sauce, hot sauce, thyme, pepper, salt and bay leaf in a large sealable plastic bag. Add the beef and seal the bag. Marinate in the refrigerator for at least 8 hours or overnight, turning occasionally. Remove the beef and reserve the marinade. Place the beef on a rack coated with nonstick cooking spray and set in a shallow roasting pan. Fold under 3 to 4 inches of the small end of the beef. Brush with the reserved marinade and discard any unused portion. Bake at 425 degrees for 35 to 40 minutes for rare (140 degrees) or 45 to 50 minutes for medium (160 degrees). Let stand for 10 minutes before slicing.
✦ Serve with small rolls and Lime Horseradish Sauce.

A new classic for elegant entertaining.

SERVES 35 TO 40

Lime Horseradish Sauce

2 tablespoons fresh lime juice
2 tablespoons prepared horseradish

1/2 cup mayonnaise

✦ Combine the lime juice, horseradish and mayonnaise in a small bowl. Stir to mix well. Cover and chill for 1 hour.

MAKES 3/4 CUP

Herbed Cheesecake

Crust

1 cup all-purpose flour
$1/2$ cup (1 stick) butter, softened
$1/2$ teaspoon salt
1 egg yolk
2 teaspoons grated lemon zest

Filling

24 ounces cream cheese, softened
2 garlic cloves, minced
1 onion, chopped
$2/3$ cup chopped fresh parsley
3 ounces Parmesan cheese,
   freshly grated
3 tablespoons all-purpose flour

4 eggs
1 teaspoon salt
$1/2$ teaspoon Tabasco sauce
2 tablespoons fresh lemon juice
1 tablespoon chopped fresh basil, or
   1 teaspoon dried basil
1 tablespoon chopped fresh tarragon,
   or 1 teaspoon dried tarragon
1 tablespoon chopped fresh oregano,
   or 1 teaspoon dried oregano
$1^{1}/2$ teaspoons chopped fresh rosemary,
   or $1/2$ teaspoon dried rosemary
$1/2$ cup chopped pepperoni
Fresh herb sprigs for garnish
Crackers

◆ *For the crust,* combine the flour, butter, salt, egg yolk and lemon zest in a bowl. Mix to form a dough. Press into the bottom and halfway up the side of an 8- or 9-inch springform pan. Freeze while preparing the filling.

◆ *For the filling,* preheat the oven to 400 degrees. Beat the cream cheese in a bowl until smooth. Beat in the garlic, onion, parsley, Parmesan cheese and flour. Add the eggs 1 at a time, beating well after each addition. Beat in the salt, Tabasco sauce, lemon juice, basil, tarragon, oregano, rosemary and pepperoni. Pour the filling into the prepared crust. Bake for 10 minutes. Reduce the heat to 325 degrees and bake for 50 minutes. Remove to a wire rack to cool. Remove ring or side and place on a serving dish or cake stand. Garnish with herb sprigs and serve with crackers.

SERVES 25 TO 30

Shrimp and Artichoke Hearts

1 egg yolk
3/4 cup olive oil
1/4 cup white wine vinegar
2 tablespoons Dijon mustard
1 shallot, finely chopped
2 tablespoons minced fresh parsley

2 tablespoons minced fresh chives
2 (14-ounce) cans artichoke hearts,
  drained
1 pound shrimp, peeled, deveined and
  cooked

◆ Beat the egg yolk in a large bowl with an electric mixer for 2 minutes. Add the olive oil, vinegar and Dijon mustard and beat until creamy. Add the shallot, parsley, chives, artichoke hearts and shrimp. Stir to coat. Cover and chill overnight.

An out-of-the-ordinary must-try marinated shrimp.

SERVES 8

Bacon-Wrapped Water Chestnuts

1 pound bacon
2 (8-ounce) cans water chestnuts,
  drained

1/4 cup green Tabasco sauce
1/2 cup mayonnaise
1/2 cup packed light brown sugar

◆ Cut the bacon slices in half and wrap each halved slice around a water chestnut. Arrange on a baking sheet with the end of the bacon against the surface of the baking sheet. Bake at 350 degrees for 45 minutes. Remove to a serving platter and keep warm.
◆ Combine the Tabasco sauce, mayonnaise and brown sugar in a small saucepan. Cook over low heat until hot, stirring frequently. Pour over the water chestnuts and serve warm.

The sauce turns this rumaki-style hors d'oeuvre into contemporary cuisine.

SERVES 20

Salmon Roll-Ups

8 ounces cream cheese, softened
3 tablespoons mayonnaise
3 tablespoons honey mustard
6 large flour tortillas
1/3 cup small capers, drained

1 head Boston lettuce
1 (1-pound) package vacuum-packed
   sliced smoked salmon
Fresh dill sprigs for garnish

◆ Beat the cream cheese, mayonnaise and honey mustard in a bowl until smooth. Spread the tortillas with the cream cheese mixture. Sprinkle with the capers.
◆ Arrange the lettuce leaves over the capers and top with the smoked salmon. Roll up the tortillas tightly and seal in plastic wrap. Chill for 5 to 6 hours. Cut each filled tortilla into 1/2-inch slices and arrange on a serving platter. Garnish each slice with a sprig of dill.

SERVES 20

Bleu Cheese Iced Grapes

1 1/3 cups finely chopped walnuts
6 ounces bleu cheese, crumbled

4 ounces cream cheese, softened
24 seedless red grapes

◆ Toast the walnuts on a baking sheet at 325 degrees for 7 to 9 minutes; let cool. Remove to a shallow bowl. Beat the bleu cheese and cream cheese in a bowl until smooth.
◆ Shape 1 tablespoon of the cheese mixture around 1 grape, enclosing it in the cheese. Repeat with the remaining grapes and cheese mixture. Chill for 15 minutes. Roll in the walnuts to coat. Chill for 30 minutes. Slice each grape in half and arrange on a serving platter. Chill until ready to serve.

An eye-catching addition to your cocktail buffet, yet so simple to prepare.

SERVES 12

Marinated Broccoli and Cauliflower

1 pound fresh broccoli,
   cut into florets
1 head cauliflower, cut into florets
1 bunch green onions, chopped
1/2 red bell pepper, chopped

1 cup mayonnaise
1/2 cup sour cream
1/4 cup Catalina salad dressing
1/4 cup tarragon vinegar
Salt and pepper to taste

◆ Combine the broccoli, cauliflower, green onions and bell pepper in a large bowl.
◆ Mix the mayonnaise, sour cream, salad dressing and vinegar in a bowl. Season with salt and pepper. Pour over the vegetables and toss to coat. Cover and chill for 24 hours.

Served with wooden picks, these zippy vegetables can replace your typical raw veggie tray. Also great as a take-along salad, serving 8 to 10.

SERVES 25 TO 30

Almond Cream-Filled Strawberries

8 ounces cream cheese, softened
1/2 cup sifted confectioners' sugar
1 teaspoon almond extract

1 quart fresh whole strawberries,
   capped

◆ Beat the cream cheese, confectioners' sugar and almond extract in a bowl until smooth. Spoon into a pastry bag fitted with a medium star tip. Chill for 1 hour.
◆ Quarter each strawberry from the tip to the stem end without cutting through the stem end. Pipe the cream cheese mixture into each strawberry.
◆ Arrange the filled strawberries on a serving plate. Chill until ready to serve.

SERVES 25 TO 30

Chocolate Pâté

1 1/2 cups half-and-half
4 ounces semisweet chocolate,
   coarsely chopped
4 ounces white chocolate,
   coarsely chopped
4 eggs, lightly beaten
2 tablespoons brandy

1 (3-ounce) package almond paste
1 cup semisweet chocolate chips
1/4 cup (1/2 stick) unsalted butter
2 tablespoons corn syrup
Sliced almonds for garnish
Shortbread cookies

◆ Preheat the oven to 350 degrees.

◆ Combine the half-and-half, semisweet chocolate and white chocolate in a saucepan. Cook over low heat until melted and smooth, stirring constantly. Let cool slightly. Stir in the eggs and brandy gradually.

◆ Line a 4×8-inch loaf pan with foil, leaving a 2-inch overhang. Pour the chocolate mixture into the loaf pan. Place the loaf pan in a larger baking pan. Add enough very hot water to the larger pan to come 1 inch up the sides of the loaf pan. Bake for 45 to 50 minutes or until a knife inserted halfway between the edge and center comes out clean. Remove to a wire rack.

◆ Roll out the almond paste between 2 sheets of waxed paper into a 4×8-inch rectangle. Remove the waxed paper and place on top of the pâté as soon as it comes out of the oven. Let cool for 1 hour. Cover and chill for at least 8 hours.

◆ Combine the chocolate chips, butter and corn syrup in a saucepan. Cook over low heat until melted and smooth, stirring constantly. Let cool. Invert the chilled pâté onto a serving plate and carefully remove the foil. Spread the chocolate glaze evenly over the top and sides. Garnish with sliced almonds and serve with shortbread cookies.

Honor your guests with this decadent dessert.

SERVES 30

Mix-and-Match Brunch for Weekend Houseguests

Ultimate Breakfast Strata and Grits Galore
or
Sausage Stroganoff Over Grits

Cinnamon Roll-Ups
or
Cream Cheese Danish
or
Orange Blossoms

Fresh Fruit Compote with Raspberry Cream
or
Hot Brandied Fruit

Visitors to Augusta love to come back again and again, and neighbors that have relocated often make an effort to come back home to the Garden City. With an itinerary packed with visiting friends, shops, and restaurants, or even a round of golf, offering a special brunch is the way to begin a spectacular weekend!

There is no better wake-up call for getting sleepyheads moving for the day than the tantalizing aroma of a brewing pot of rich coffee. Serve freshly squeezed juice garnished with fruit, mint ice cubes, or ginger as a special touch. Do you have a penchant for Champagne? Perhaps the bubbles of Mimosas or Bellinis will do the trick. Choose your favorites to accompany these versatile brunch menus.

Vivid colors and savory flavor make the strata truly the ultimate breakfast entrée, and the mix-and-match grits and pastry choices combine as delightful Southern and sweet favorites. Choose the Fresh Fruit Compote with Raspberry Cream or Hot Brandied Fruit, depending on the season.

Spend the day basking in the company of friends, and you'll be refreshed and looking forward to the week ahead—and perhaps next weekend's guests!

Ultimate Breakfast Strata

1 tablespoon extra-virgin olive oil
10 ounces breakfast sausage patties
6 to 8 slices French bread, cut into
   1-inch cubes (about 4 cups)
9 eggs
3 cups milk
1/2 cup chopped green onions
1 pound fresh asparagus, trimmed and
   cut into 1-inch pieces

2 roasted red bell peppers, peeled,
   seeded and thinly sliced
2 cups (8 ounces) shredded fontina
   cheese
Salt and pepper to taste
1 cup (4 ounces) shredded fontina
   cheese

◆ Heat the olive oil in a skillet over medium heat. Add the sausage and fry until cooked through, turning occasionally. Remove to paper towels to drain. Let cool and cut into thin slices.

◆ Combine the cooked sausage and bread cubes in a large bowl. Whisk the eggs and milk in a bowl. Pour over the bread and sausage. Add the green onions, asparagus, roasted bell peppers and 2 cups cheese. Season with salt and pepper and stir to mix. Pour into a greased 9×13-inch baking dish. Cover and chill for at least 4 hours or overnight. Bring to room temperature.

◆ Preheat the oven to 350 degrees. Bake the strata for 1 hour or until the top is golden brown and a knife inserted in the center comes out clean. Sprinkle 1 cup cheese over the top. Bake for 1 minute longer or until the cheese melts. Remove to a wire rack and let stand for 10 minutes before serving.

Assembling in advance makes this recipe ideal for entertaining.

SERVES 8

Grits Galore

4 cups water
1¹/3 cups milk
1¹/2 cups quick-cooking grits
4 ounces cream cheese
1 cup (4 ounces) shredded
   Cheddar cheese

8 slices bacon, crisp-cooked and
   crumbled
1 (10-ounce) can tomatoes with
   green chiles
Additional crumbled cooked bacon
   for garnish

◆ Combine the water and milk in a 2-quart saucepan. Bring to a boil and stir in the grits. Return to a boil. Reduce the heat and cover. Simmer for 5 to 7 minutes, adding more water if needed.

◆ Add the cream cheese and Cheddar cheese. Cook until the cheeses melt, stirring constantly. Stir in the bacon and tomatoes with green chiles. Spoon into a serving bowl and garnish with crumbled bacon. Serve immediately.

Savory, spicy, and so good!

SERVES 6 TO 8

Sausage Stroganoff Over Grits

2 tablespoons butter
2 large onions, chopped
1 pound fresh mushrooms, chopped
1 garlic clove, minced
2 pounds hot country bulk
  pork sausage
3 tablespoons all-purpose flour

2 cups milk
2 tablespoons Worcestershire sauce
2 teaspoons soy sauce
Salt and pepper to taste
1 cup sour cream
Hot cooked grits or biscuits

◆ Melt the butter in a skillet. Add the onions, mushrooms and garlic and sauté until the vegetables are tender. Remove from the heat.

◆ Brown the sausage in a large saucepan, stirring until crumbly; drain. Stir in the flour. Add the milk and simmer until slightly thickened, stirring frequently.

◆ Add the sautéed vegetables, Worcestershire sauce and soy sauce. Season with salt and pepper and stir to mix. Simmer for 10 minutes. Can be frozen at this point.

◆ Stir in the sour cream just before serving. Serve over cooked grits or biscuits.

Freezes well to keep on hand for a relaxed weekend breakfast.

SERVES 10

Cinnamon Roll-Ups

24 slices firm white sandwich bread,
  crusts removed
8 ounces cream cheese, softened
1 egg yolk

1 1/4 cups sugar
1 tablespoon cinnamon
1/2 cup (1 stick) unsalted butter,
  melted

◆ Roll the bread slices flat with a rolling pin or press with hands.

◆ Mix the cream cheese, egg yolk and 1/4 cup of the sugar in a bowl. Spread about 1 tablespoon on each bread slice and roll up tightly.

◆ Mix the remaining 1 cup sugar and the cinnamon in a shallow bowl. Brush each roll-up with melted butter and roll in the cinnamon-sugar. Arrange on a baking sheet. Chill or freeze for at least 2 hours.

◆ Preheat the oven to 400 degrees. Bake for 9 to 12 minutes or until golden brown. Serve warm.

These can be frozen for up to two months before baking.

SERVES 12

Because the Masters® is golf's only major championship with a permanent home, players are reunited with Augusta National's undulations, greens, trees, creeks, bunkers, and ponds every spring. Yet they know that they can't take that familiarity for granted. "At Augusta, you'll learn something every time you play it for the rest of your life."

—Ben Crenshaw, two-time Masters® Champion (1984, 1995)

Cream Cheese Danish

2 (8-ounce) cans refrigerator
   crescent rolls
16 ounces cream cheese, softened

3/4 cup sugar
1 teaspoon vanilla extract
1 egg white, lightly beaten

◆ Preheat the oven to 350 degrees.
◆ Unroll 1 can of the crescent roll dough and press onto the bottom of an ungreased 7×11-inch baking dish, pressing the seams to seal.
◆ Mix the cream cheese, sugar and vanilla in a bowl. Spread over the dough in the baking dish. Unroll the remaining can of crescent roll dough and press the seams to seal. Place on top of the cheese layer. Brush with the egg white.
◆ Bake for 25 to 30 minutes. Remove to a wire rack and let cool slightly.

SERVES 8 TO 10

DURING THE FIRST TWO YEARS THE COURSE WAS OPEN, AUGUSTA NATIONAL'S FIRST NINE WAS ITS SECOND NINE AND VICE VERSA. THE INITIAL MASTERS® TOURNAMENT, HELD IN 1934, WAS PLAYED IN ITS ORIGINAL ORDER. BUT WHEN THE CLUB REOPENED IN THE FALL OF THAT SAME YEAR, THE NINES WERE SWITCHED.

Orange Blossoms

Muffins

1 (2-layer) package yellow cake mix
4 eggs
1 (3-ounce) package lemon instant
  pudding mix
3/4 cup orange juice
3/4 cup vegetable oil

Glaze

2 tablespoons vegetable oil
1/3 cup plus 2 tablespoons orange
  juice
2 cups confectioners' sugar

◆ *For the muffins,* preheat the oven to 350 degrees. Combine the cake mix, eggs, pudding mix, orange juice and oil in a large bowl. Stir to mix well. Spoon into miniature muffin cups coated with nonstick cooking spray. Bake for 8 to 10 minutes or until a wooden pick inserted in the center comes out clean. Cool in the pans for 5 minutes. Remove to a wire rack to cool completely.

◆ *For the glaze,* mix the oil, orange juice and confectioners' sugar in a bowl. Dip the tops of the cooled muffins in the glaze. Set upright on a wire rack or waxed paper to let the glaze set.

—BONNIE MIZE, WIFE OF LARRY MIZE

"They have a very light flavor. My family cannot stop eating these!"

MAKES ABOUT 36 MINIATURE MUFFINS

"THE MASTERS® TOURNAMENT HAS ALWAYS BEEN VERY SPECIAL TO ME. GROWING UP IN AUGUSTA AND EXPERIENCING THE EXCITEMENT EVERY YEAR OF THE PROFESSIONALS COMING TO TOWN MOTIVATED ME TO PURSUE GOLF AS A CAREER. PLAYING IN THE TOURNAMENT WAS A DREAM COME TRUE, AND THEN WINNING IN 1987, IS STILL THE HIGHLIGHT OF MY CAREER AND A WONDERFUL MEMORY."

—LARRY MIZE, MASTERS® CHAMPION (1987)

Fresh Fruit Compote with Raspberry Cream

8 ounces cream cheese, softened
1 (7-ounce) jar marshmallow creme
12 ounces whipped topping
1/4 cup raspberry liqueur
1 cantaloupe, peeled, seeded and cut
　　into bite-size pieces
1 honeydew melon, peeled, seeded
　　and cut into bite-size pieces

1 pineapple, peeled, cored and cut
　　into bite-size pieces
2 cups fresh raspberries, strawberries,
　　blueberries, kiwifruit or sliced
　　peaches

◆ Beat the cream cheese and marshmallow creme in a bowl with an electric mixer at low speed until blended. Fold in the whipped topping. Fold in the liqueur.

◆ Layer the fruit and cream in a trifle bowl in 6 layers, starting with the heavier fruit and ending with the cream.

*The cream, with or without the liqueur, makes a
divine dip for any kind of fruit.*

SERVES 8 TO 12

Hot Brandied Fruit

1 (30-ounce) can apricot halves
1 (29-ounce) can pear halves
1 (20-ounce) can sliced peaches
1 (20-ounce) can pineapple chunks
1 (10-ounce) jar maraschino cherries
1/2 cup (1 stick) margarine

3/4 cup packed brown sugar
1/2 cup brandy
10 whole cloves
4 cinnamon sticks
1/4 teaspoon ground cinnamon

◆ Drain the fruit, reserving 1 cup of the combined fruit juices.
◆ Arrange the drained apricot halves, pear halves, sliced peaches, pineapple chunks and maraschino cherries in a 9×13-inch baking dish.
◆ Combine the margarine and brown sugar in a small saucepan. Cook over medium-low heat until melted and smooth, stirring often. Stir in the reserved fruit juice, brandy, cloves, cinnamon sticks and ground cinnamon. Pour over the fruit in the baking dish. Cover and chill overnight. Bring to room temperature.
◆ Preheat the oven to 350 degrees. Bake for 30 minutes or until bubbly.

SERVES 10

Lounging at the Lake,
A Family Fourth of July

Crab and Corn-Filled Endive
Peach Salsa
Honey Lime Grilled Chicken
Grilled Summer Vegetables Over Orzo Pilaf
Fruity Spinach Salad with
Honey Poppy Seed Dressing
Green Bean and Potato Salad
Cream Cheese Pecan Pie

Thousands of miles of pine-rimmed shoreline can be reached within minutes of Augusta, and local families take full advantage—especially during the summer months. The Savannah River lakes of Thurmond, Russell, and Hartwell were developed during the 1940s and 1950s by the U.S. Army Corps of Engineers and provide a multitude of fishing, boating, camping, and other water-sport opportunities in Georgia and South Carolina.

Whether you're entertaining at a private lake house or visiting a recreational area, treat your crowd to this healthy menu brimming with robust summer flavors. After a day spent skiing, swimming, or relaxing dockside, begin and end your meal with the classic Georgia ingredients in Peach Salsa and Cream Cheese Pecan Pie. Fruity Spinach Salad and the dazzling array of grilled vegetables over orzo complement the Honey Lime Grilled Chicken.

Decorating for your all-American feast should not be a lot of trouble—nor do you have to buy holiday-specific merchandise. Pull red, white, and blue accents from around your home, and remember the stars and stripes!

Reunion time or not, the Fourth of July is a prime occasion for taking an annual family group photo. In later years, you will be pleased to have captured these relaxed moments, which complement collections of more formal group shots from weddings and Christmas.

Ensure that all guests perform their patriotic duty by assigning workstations—at the grill, in the kitchen, and cleanup patrol. With the mission of a leisurely day at the lake complete, ready your crowd after sunset to admire the fireworks display!

Crab and Corn-Filled Endive

8 ounces fresh crab meat, drained
  and flaked
1 cup frozen yellow corn kernels,
  thawed
1/2 cup finely chopped red onion
1/4 cup mayonnaise
2 1/2 tablespoons chopped fresh
  thyme, parsley or chervil
2 tablespoons chopped fresh chives

2 tablespoons frozen orange juice
  concentrate, thawed
2 tablespoons fresh lemon juice
1/2 teaspoon cumin
1/8 teaspoon cayenne pepper
Salt and pepper to taste
4 heads Belgian endive, separated
  into leaves

◆ Combine the crab meat, corn, onion, mayonnaise, thyme, chives, orange juice concentrate, lemon juice, cumin and cayenne pepper in a bowl. Season with salt and pepper. Stir to mix well. Cover and chill for up to 24 hours.

◆ Fill the base end of each endive leaf with 1 heaping tablespoon of the crab meat mixture. Serve immediately.

Cool, crisp, and pretty on a platter.

SERVES 10

IT WAS IN AUGUSTA THAT "ARNIE'S ARMY" BEGAN TO TAKE SHAPE WHILE ARNOLD PALMER WAS WINNING HIS FIRST MASTERS® IN 1958.

Peach Salsa

3 peaches, peeled, pitted and cut into
  bite-size pieces
1 red or green bell pepper, diced
1/4 cup diced red onion
2 tablespoons fresh lime juice

5 to 6 fresh basil leaves, cut with
  scissors into ribbons
1/2 teaspoon minced garlic
1/4 teaspoon salt

✦ Combine the peaches, bell pepper, onion, lime juice, basil, garlic and salt in a bowl. Stir to mix well. Cover and chill for at least 1 hour.

Best made at the peak of the peach season.

SERVES 8

Honey Lime Grilled Chicken

Juice of 1 lime
2 tablespoons honey
2 tablespoons olive oil
1 1/2 teaspoons finely chopped
  fresh cilantro

1 rounded teaspoon cumin
4 to 6 boneless skinless chicken
  breasts
1/2 teaspoon salt
1/2 teaspoon pepper

✦ Whisk the lime juice, honey, olive oil, cilantro and cumin in a small bowl.
✦ Arrange the chicken in a shallow dish. Sprinkle with salt and pepper. Pour the lime mixture over the chicken and turn to coat. Cover and marinate in the refrigerator for at least 4 hours.
✦ Remove the chicken and discard the marinade. Grill the chicken until cooked through.

*These can also be served as sandwiches with your favorite topping;
try slices of avocado or salsa verde.*

SERVES 4 TO 6

Grilled Summer Vegetables Over Orzo Pilaf

6 cups low-sodium chicken broth	4 Roma tomatoes, halved and seeded
2 cups orzo	3 tablespoons olive oil
2 teaspoons chopped fresh rosemary	1 tablespoon cider vinegar
Extra-virgin olive oil	1/2 teaspoon chopped fresh parsley
1 large red onion, cut into	1/2 teaspoon chopped fresh thyme
1/2-inch slices	1/2 teaspoon chopped fresh rosemary
3 yellow squash, halved lengthwise	1/4 teaspoon kosher salt
3 zucchini, halved lengthwise	1/4 cup crumbled goat cheese

◆ Combine the broth, orzo and 2 teaspoons rosemary in a saucepan. Bring to a simmer over medium-low heat. Cook for 25 minutes or until the liquid is absorbed. Remove from the heat.

◆ Brush extra-virgin olive oil on the onion, yellow squash, zucchini and tomatoes. Grill for 5 minutes or until tender, turning the onion, yellow squash and zucchini once. Grill the tomatoes skin side down and do not turn during grilling.

◆ Remove the vegetables to a work surface. Cut into bite-size pieces.

◆ Whisk the olive oil, vinegar, parsley, thyme, 1/2 teaspoon rosemary and the salt in a large bowl. Add the grilled vegetables and toss gently to coat. Spread the cooked orzo on a serving platter. Top with the undrained grilled vegetables and sprinkle with the goat cheese.

A versatile recipe that you can use with any grilled vegetable you prefer. Try mushrooms, peppers, or eggplant.

SERVES 10 TO 12

Fruity Spinach Salad
with Honey Poppy Seed Dressing

1/2 cup low-fat mayonnaise

3 tablespoons honey

1 tablespoon lemon juice

1 tablespoon poppy seeds

1 pint strawberries, quartered

1 (10-ounce) bag pre-washed spinach, torn into bite-size pieces

1 grapefruit, peeled, sectioned and cut into bite-size pieces

2 tablespoons toasted pecans

◆ Whisk the mayonnaise, honey, lemon juice and poppy seeds in a small bowl.

◆ Combine the strawberries, spinach and grapefruit in a large bowl. Add the dressing and toss to coat. Sprinkle with the pecans just before serving.

Grapefruit and strawberries make this salad refreshing on a hot summer day.

SERVES 4 TO 6

Green Bean and Potato Salad

2 pounds red-skinned new potatoes, cut into thick wedges
3 cups fresh green beans, trimmed and cut in half
6 tablespoons olive oil
2 tablespoons balsamic vinegar
2 teaspoons crushed garlic
1/2 teaspoon salt
1/2 teaspoon pepper
1 tablespoon Dijon mustard
3 green onions, chopped
1 cup chopped fresh basil leaves

◆ Cook the potatoes and green beans separately in water to cover just until tender, 6 to 7 minutes. Drain and rinse the vegetables.
◆ Combine the potatoes and beans in a large bowl. Whisk the olive oil, vinegar and garlic in a small bowl. Whisk in the salt, pepper and Dijon mustard.
◆ Pour over the potatoes and beans. Add the green onions and basil and toss gently to mix. Cover and chill for 2 hours.

Vinaigrette and fresh vegetables make this version unlike your everyday potato salad.

SERVES 8 TO 10

TEN CABINS ARE LOCATED ON AUGUSTA NATIONAL GROUNDS. SEVEN WHITE CABINS FORM A SEMICIRCLE EAST OF THE WOODS BORDERING THE TENTH FAIRWAY. THE EISENHOWER, BUTLER, AND ROBERTS CABINS STAND ALONE.

Cream Cheese Pecan Pie

1 (2-crust) refrigerator pie pastry
8 ounces cream cheese, softened
1 egg
$1/2$ cup sugar
1 teaspoon vanilla extract
$1/4$ teaspoon salt

1 cup chopped pecans
1 cup light corn syrup
3 eggs
$1/4$ cup sugar
1 teaspoon vanilla extract

◆ Preheat the oven to 350 degrees.
◆ Stack the 2 pie pastries on a work surface and roll or press together with hands. Fit into a 9-inch pie plate. Fold the edges under and crimp.
◆ Combine the cream cheese, 1 egg, $1/2$ cup sugar, 1 teaspoon vanilla and the salt in a bowl. Beat with an electric mixer until smooth. Pour into the prepared crust. Sprinkle with the pecans.
◆ Combine the corn syrup, 3 eggs, $1/4$ cup sugar and 1 teaspoon vanilla in a bowl. Stir to mix well. Pour over the pecans.
◆ Bake for 50 to 60 minutes or until set. Remove to a wire rack to cool.

Almost like a cheesecake but with pecan pie on top.

SERVES 8

Date Night Dinner for Two

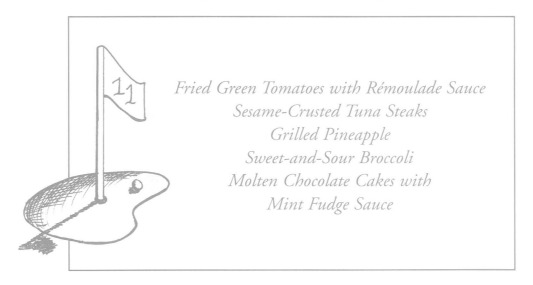

Fried Green Tomatoes with Rémoulade Sauce
Sesame-Crusted Tuna Steaks
Grilled Pineapple
Sweet-and-Sour Broccoli
Molten Chocolate Cakes with
Mint Fudge Sauce

You needn't always go out for a romantic dinner—all you need is an inviting outdoor setting, flickering candlelight, and soft strains of sentimental music to create the ambiance that this meal commands.

Augusta's climate lends itself to warm evenings with the sun shining late into the afternoons, so we have long taken advantage of its generosity by serving dinner alfresco style. Relying on favorite Augusta, Georgia, restaurant chefs, we encourage you to indulge your senses at home with these menu selections.

An intimate table sized just for two is a must for getting close. For a beautiful effect, try layering your tablecloths. Start with a plain cloth in a favorite color, then top with a smaller, square cloth in a complementary shade. Using sheer fabric or tulle provides a softer effect for a romantic, pampered feeling.

Adorn your table with beautiful details—tie a pretty ribbon around each napkin and add one perfect flower under the bow. A centerpiece of luscious, ripe fruit in a crystal bowl can be a lovely yet practical alternative to flowers; aim for colorful abundance and choose whatever looks most appealing. This centerpiece can be a delicious accompaniment to Champagne or sparkling wine.

For an uncomplicated yet charming look, fill two small bud vases with a few rosebuds or other beloved flowers, adding a sprig of greenery such as ivy or galyx. Set one vase in front of each place setting.

As you attend to the final details, be sure to choose the appropriate music to accompany your meal. Will you select nostalgic love songs, soothing undertones, or just something flirtatious? Choose to burn unscented candles during dinner so as not to compete with the sensuous smells of the food. Keep the lighting subdued. An area that is lit with only candles can be completely enchanting.

Fried Green Tomatoes with Rémoulade Sauce

3 green tomatoes
1 egg, lightly beaten
1/2 cup buttermilk
1/2 cup all-purpose flour
1 teaspoon each salt and pepper

1 cup finely crushed herb-seasoned
  stuffing mix
Vegetable oil for frying
Salt and pepper to taste
Rémoulade Sauce (below)

◆ Cut the green tomatoes into 1/3-inch slices. Mix the egg and buttermilk in a shallow dish. Mix the flour, 1 teaspoon salt and 1 teaspoon pepper in a shallow dish. Spread the stuffing crumbs in a shallow dish. Dredge the tomato slices in the flour mixture. Dip in the egg mixture and then in the stuffing crumbs to coat.

◆ Heat oil to 375 degrees in a cast-iron skillet. Add the tomatoes and cook for 2 minutes per side or until golden brown. Drain on paper towels and season with salt and pepper while hot. Serve with Rémoulade Sauce and steamed shrimp on a bed of mixed greens.

SERVES 4 TO 6

Rémoulade Sauce

2 cups mayonnaise
1 cup sour cream
1 1/4 cups chili sauce
1/2 cup Dijon mustard

1/4 cup prepared horseradish
2 scallions, finely chopped
1 rib celery, finely chopped
Salt and pepper to taste

◆ Mix the mayonnaise, sour cream, chili sauce, Dijon mustard, horseradish, scallions and celery in a bowl. Season with salt and pepper. Stir to mix well. Cover and chill for at least 1 hour.

—CALVERT'S

MAKES 5 1/2 CUPS

Sesame-Crusted Tuna Steaks

1 cup soy sauce
2 tablespoons chopped fresh ginger
1/4 cup chopped green onions
1/4 cup packed brown sugar
2 to 4 tuna steaks

Mixed black and white toasted sesame
  seeds for coating
Hot mashed cooked potatoes or
  wasabi sauce and pickled ginger

◆ Combine the soy sauce, fresh ginger, green onions and brown sugar in a saucepan. Bring to a boil and cook until the sugar dissolves, stirring often. Strain and let cool.

◆ Arrange the tuna steaks in a shallow dish. Pour the cooled soy sauce mixture over the tuna and turn to coat. Cover and marinate in the refrigerator for at least 8 hours.

◆ Remove the tuna and discard the marinade. Coat 1 side of each steak with sesame seeds. Sear in a hot skillet, seeded side down, for 1 to 2 minutes. Turn and cook to desired doneness. Serve over mashed potatoes or with wasabi sauce and pickled ginger.

—FRENCH MARKET GRILLE

SERVES 2 TO 4

SAM SNEAD SAID IN 1951 THAT AUGUSTA WAS "THE ONLY COURSE I EVER PLAYED WHERE YOU COULD HEAR THE BALL ROLLING ON THE GREENS. THEY'RE SO SLICK THE BALL SOUNDS LIKE IT'S FRYING."

Grilled Pineapple

1/4 cup reduced-sodium teriyaki sauce
2 teaspoons vegetable oil
2 tablespoons brown sugar

1 pineapple, peeled, cored and cut
  into 8 rings

◆ Mix the teriyaki sauce, oil and brown sugar in a 9×13-inch baking dish. Add the pineapple rings and turn to coat. Let marinate for 1 hour. Remove the pineapple and discard the marinade.
◆ Place the pineapple on a grill pan coated with nonstick cooking spray. Cover the grill and cook for 2 minutes per side or until lightly browned and tender.

SERVES 6 TO 8

Sweet-and-Sour Broccoli

1 tablespoon sugar
1 tablespoon light soy sauce
2 teaspoons rice wine vinegar

1 pound fresh broccoli, cut into spears
1 tablespoon toasted sesame seeds
  (optional)

◆ Combine the sugar, soy sauce and vinegar in a small saucepan. Cook until the sugar dissolves, stirring often. Simmer for 1 minute. Remove from the heat and keep warm.
◆ Cook the broccoli in a steamer basket over boiling water for 5 minutes or until tender-crisp. Remove to a bowl. Add the soy sauce mixture and toss to coat. Sprinkle with the sesame seeds.

This light sauce adds zing to fresh steamed broccoli.

SERVES 6

Molten Chocolate Cakes with Mint Fudge Sauce

Sauce

4 1/2 ounces bittersweet chocolate,
   chopped
2 ounces unsweetened chocolate,
   chopped
1/3 cup hot water
1/4 cup light corn syrup
3/4 teaspoon peppermint extract

Cakes

5 ounces bittersweet chocolate,
   chopped
10 tablespoons unsalted butter
3 eggs
3 egg yolks
1 1/4 cups confectioners' sugar
1/2 cup all-purpose flour
Ice cream
Fresh mint sprigs for garnish

◆ *For the sauce,* combine the bittersweet chocolate and unsweetened chocolate in the top of a double boiler. Cook over barely simmering water until melted, stirring often. Add the hot water, corn syrup and peppermint extract and whisk until smooth. Remove from the heat and let cool slightly.

◆ *For the cakes,* preheat the oven to 450 degrees. Combine the chocolate and butter in a heavy medium saucepan. Cook over low heat until melted, stirring often. Remove from the heat and let cool slightly. Whisk the eggs and egg yolks in a large bowl. Whisk in the confectioners' sugar. Whisk in the chocolate mixture gradually. Whisk in the flour. Pour into 6 buttered 3/4-cup soufflé or custard cups. Bake for 11 minutes or until the sides are set but the center remains soft and liquid. Run a knife around the inside of the cups to loosen the cakes. Invert immediately onto serving plates. Spoon the sauce around the cakes. Serve with ice cream and garnish with mint sprigs.

—CALVERT'S

*Splurge with your sweetheart with this sensuous dessert from
one of Augusta's finest restaurants.*

SERVES 6

Back-to-School Bash

Oven-Baked Chicken Strips
Cheesy Mac n' Cheese
Speedy Green Beans
Tangy Apple Salad
Popcorn Treats
Too-Good-to-Be-True Cookies

"Playing School" is a well-loved childhood game and a terrific theme for a children's party! Banish any back-to-school angst by hosting a party to ease your children back into a normal routine. Encourage their excitement about seeing old friends, making new ones, and meeting their teacher. Invite playmates from the neighborhood and classmates from last year that they haven't seen all summer.

Both younger and older children will have fun rotating through activity centers—just like school! Bob for apples, decorate a pencil holder made from empty juice or soup cans, browse through last year's annual, and play ABC or math flash-card games. The centers can be as simple as you like, and a bell or timer can be the signal to switch to the next center. Set out spelling board games, memory match cards, or coloring sheets, and have your little guests make their own flash-card games.

After all the children have arrived and have had a chance to finish center time, it is time for the "school day" to begin. In keeping with a typical morning, recite the pledge of allegiance and take attendance of the partygoers. To really get into the spirit of the party, the "teacher" should wear spectacles, use a pointer, and have a notebook handy.

Don't forget to take lunch orders while calling roll, asking whether each student wants "brought lunch" or "bought lunch." Serve brown-bag style to those who order a "brought lunch," items such as a peanut butter and jelly sandwich, apple or box of raisins, maybe even carrot sticks, a bag of chips, juice box, and don't forget the homemade cookie (see the recipe for our Too-Good-to-Be-True Cookies). For those who want a "bought lunch," serve our yummy hot lunch menu on trays or divided plates. After lunch hour, the children can separate into teams for a school supply scavenger hunt. End the school day with a sack of treats. Everyone loves receiving new pencils and erasers, markers, or even a ruler. After a fun day of going "back-to-school," your students will be ready and excited for the rush of fall to begin.

Oven-Baked Chicken Strips

3 tablespoons butter, melted
1 tablespoon soy sauce
1 cup crushed sesame crackers
1 teaspoon ginger

1/4 teaspoon salt
1 pound boneless skinless chicken
  breasts, cut into strips

◆ Preheat the oven to 450 degrees.
◆ Mix the melted butter and soy sauce in a shallow dish. Mix the crushed crackers, ginger and salt in a shallow dish.
◆ Dip the chicken strips in the butter mixture and then in the crushed crackers to coat. Arrange on a baking sheet coated with nonstick cooking spray.
◆ Bake for 10 minutes or until cooked through.

A home-baked healthy alternative to a fast-food favorite.

SERVES 6

"PAPA, TRUST YOUR SWING."—THE MESSAGE SCRIBBLED ON VIJAY SINGH'S BAG BY 10-YEAR-OLD SON QASS THE NIGHT BEFORE SINGH'S VICTORIOUS ROUND OF THE MASTERS® IN 2000.

Cheesy Mac 'n Cheese

8 ounces elbow macaroni
3 tablespoons butter, softened
4 ounces Velveeta cheese,
cut into cubes
3 ounces cream cheese, softened
and cut into cubes

1 (8-ounce) package shredded
Monterey Jack and Cheddar cheese
1 egg
1 cup heavy cream
Salt and pepper to taste
Seasoned salt to taste

◆ Preheat the oven to 350 degrees.
◆ Cook the macaroni according to the package directions. Rinse with hot water and drain well. Place the hot macaroni in a large bowl. Add the butter and stir until the butter melts. Stir in the Velveeta cheese, cream cheese and Monterey Jack and Cheddar cheese.
◆ Whisk the egg and cream in a bowl. Season with salt, pepper and seasoned salt. Add to the macaroni mixture and stir to mix well. Pour into a baking dish coated with nonstick cooking spray.
◆ Bake for 30 minutes, stirring once halfway through baking.

SERVES 6 TO 8

"WHEN I WAS A BOY, I WAS NOT ALLOWED TO PLAY THE LOCAL GOLF COURSE DURING THE DAY, SO I WOULD GO OUT JUST BEFORE NIGHTTIME."
—SEVE BALLESTEROS, TWO-TIME MASTERS® CHAMPION (1980, 1983)

Speedy Green Beans

2¹/2 tablespoons olive oil
2 teaspoons minced garlic
2 pounds frozen green beans

2 chicken bouillon cubes
1 (14-ounce) can diced tomatoes, drained

◆ Heat the olive oil in a large saucepan over medium-high heat, tilting the saucepan to coat. Add the garlic and sauté until almost starting to brown. Stir in the frozen beans and bouillon cubes.

◆ Reduce the heat to medium. Cook, uncovered, for 9 to 10 minutes, stirring occasionally. Cover and cook for 4 minutes. Reduce the heat if all the liquid is evaporating. Stir in the tomatoes and turn off the heat. Cover and let stand until ready to serve.

Weeknight preparation, weekend flavor!

SERVES 4 TO 6

Tangy Apple Salad

3 tablespoons orange-flavored drink mix
3 cups diced cored Red Delicious apples

1 cup miniature marshmallows
1 (8-ounce) can crushed pineapple
1/2 cup raisins
1/2 cup nuts (optional)

◆ Sprinkle the drink mix over the apples in a bowl. Toss to coat. Add the marshmallows, pineapple, raisins and nuts. Stir to mix well. Cover and chill for at least 1 hour.

SERVES 6 TO 8

Popcorn Treats

1/2 cup (1 stick) butter
1 (10-ounce) package marshmallows
4 quarts popped popcorn

1 (16-ounce) package candy-coated
  chocolate pieces
2 cups salted peanuts (optional)

◆ Melt the butter and marshmallows in a large saucepan over low heat, stirring occasionally. Add the popcorn, chocolate pieces and peanuts and stir to mix well. Press into a buttered 9×13-inch baking pan. Cut into squares when cool.

A different take on Rice Krispies Treats.

SERVES 15 TO 18

Too-Good-to-Be-True Cookies

1 cup (2 sticks) butter, softened
3/4 cup packed light brown sugar
3/4 cup granulated sugar
1 teaspoon vanilla extract
1 egg

1 1/2 cups rolled oats
1 1/2 cups self-rising flour
1 cup dried cranberries, chopped
1 (8-ounce) package toffee bits
1 cup semisweet chocolate chips

◆ Preheat the oven to 350 degrees.
◆ Beat the butter, brown sugar and granulated sugar in a bowl until light and fluffy. Add the vanilla and egg and stir to mix well. Stir in the oats, flour, cranberries, toffee bits and chocolate chips. Drop by teaspoonfuls on a greased baking sheet.
◆ Bake for 10 minutes. Remove to a wire rack and let cool before removing from the baking sheet.

Every ingredient you love in a cookie all stirred into one.

MAKES 3 DOZEN COOKIES

Strolling Through Summerville,
A Progressive Dinner

Baked Garlic and Sun-Dried Tomato Spread
Olive Cups
Scallop Shooters in Saffron Cream
Summer Wine
Lentil and Lemon Soup
You Thought You Didn't Like Lamb Chops
Greek Chicken
Greek Salad
Almond Raisin Rice
Artichoke Spinach Pinwheels
Citrus Trifle

Augusta's Summerville neighborhood provides the backdrop each October for a fabulous tour of homes. While the neighborhood dates back to the early 1800s, the majority of Summerville's homes were built in the resort era of the early 1900s and represent an eclectic blend of architecture. Situated on higher ground, the breezy Hill area offered some relief from the heat common to the lower lands bordering the Savannah River. Mediterranean architecture was a popular style for this resort area of Augusta, because the designs are based on keeping the home cool.

A progressive dinner planned with good friends can be your own "tour of homes." The occasion may feature the chance to see seasonal decorations or may just be an opportunity for a leisurely evening.

Just as the revival styles of architecture combine glimpses of other cultures, our menu offers an interpretation of favorite Mediterranean ingredients with unique presentations.

The progressive format divides preparation among each host home, allowing each stop to offer a memorable course. Antipasti served with cool Summer Wine begins the progression. Next, the entrée course allows the Greek Chicken to cook in the oven as the lamb chops are finished on the grill. True to the Mediterranean tradition of serving fruit for dessert, the gorgeous Citrus Trifle is a light and refreshing finale. If time and the number of homes allows, the soup course is worthy of its own stop!

Baked Garlic and Sun-Dried Tomato Spread

4 large garlic bulbs, peeled and
   cloves separated
1/4 cup olive oil
2 cups sun-dried tomatoes
   (not oil-packed)
3/4 tablespoon fines herbes

2 to 2 1/2 cups chicken broth
2 1/2 tablespoons butter, thinly sliced
6 ounces goat cheese, sliced
Fresh basil leaves
1 large loaf Italian bread, sliced

◆ Preheat the oven to 375 degrees.
◆ Spread the garlic cloves in a 9×9-inch baking dish. Drizzle the olive oil over the garlic and top with the tomatoes. Sprinkle with the fines herbes. Add 2 cups broth and dot with the butter.
◆ Bake for 1 hour or until the garlic and tomatoes are tender, basting with the pan juices every 15 minutes. Add more broth if all the liquid is evaporating.
◆ Arrange the cheese slices on top. Bake for 10 minutes longer or until the cheese is almost melted. Sprinkle basil over the top.
◆ To serve, spread a garlic clove on a slice of bread and top with some of the melted cheese and tomato mixture.
◆ *Note: Leftovers get a new life as a cold appetizer by mixing 1/3 to 1/2 cup of the leftover mixture, 1 cup cream cheese and 8 to 10 chopped fresh basil leaves in a bowl. Spread on crackers.*

SERVES 12

Olive Cups

1 cup chopped pecans

1 cup (4 ounces) shredded Cheddar
  cheese

1/2 cup pimento-stuffed green olives,
  sliced

1/2 cup black olives, chopped

2 tablespoons mayonnaise

2 (15-count) packages miniature
  phyllo shells

◆ Preheat the oven to 350 degrees.

◆ Combine the pecans, cheese, green olives, black olives and mayonnaise in a bowl. Stir to mix well.

◆ Fill the phyllo shells with the olive mixture. Arrange on a baking sheet.

◆ Bake for 8 minutes or until the cheese melts. Serve immediately.

A blend of tangy olives and crunchy pecans in an easy to eat phyllo cup.

SERVES 30

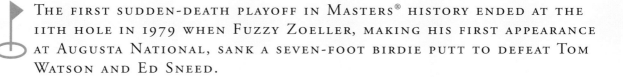

THE FIRST SUDDEN-DEATH PLAYOFF IN MASTERS® HISTORY ENDED AT THE 11TH HOLE IN 1979 WHEN FUZZY ZOELLER, MAKING HIS FIRST APPEARANCE AT AUGUSTA NATIONAL, SANK A SEVEN-FOOT BIRDIE PUTT TO DEFEAT TOM WATSON AND ED SNEED.

Scallop Shooters in Saffron Cream

1/2 teaspoon saffron threads
Juice of 1 lemon
6 tablespoons sour cream
1 tablespoon heavy cream, half-and-half or milk
Salt and pepper to taste

1 pound (about 30 large) sea scallops, rinsed and patted dry
Adobo seasoning or seasoned salt
1 tablespoon olive oil
Saffron threads for garnish

◆ Combine 1/2 teaspoon saffron and the lemon juice in a small saucepan. Bring to a simmer. Strain into a bowl. Whisk in the sour cream and heavy cream. Season with salt and pepper. Keep warm.
◆ Preheat a range-top or outdoor grill on High for 5 minutes.
◆ Season the scallops with adobo seasoning in a bowl. Add the olive oil and toss to coat. Grill the scallops for 3 to 4 minutes per side or just until tender.
◆ Remove the scallops to shot glasses and top each with a dollop of the saffron cream. Garnish each with a saffron thread. Arrange on a serving platter.

A delectable novelty for dinner and cocktail parties.

MAKES 30 SERVINGS

Summer Wine

1 (750-milliliter) bottle dry white wine	Ice cubes
1 cup dry marsala	1 cup chilled club soda or sparkling mineral water
1/4 cup Cognac or brandy	Thin slices cucumber, halved, for garnish
1 cup superfine sugar	
2 to 4 lemons, thinly sliced	Thin slices lemon, halved, for garnish
1/2 to 1 cucumber, thinly sliced	

◆ Combine the white wine, marsala, Cognac and sugar in a large pitcher or punch bowl. Stir until the sugar dissolves.

◆ Stir in the lemon slices, cucumber slices and ice cubes. Stir in the club soda. Serve immediately in chilled wine glasses or highball glasses, garnished with a half slice of cucumber and half slice of lemon.

◆ *Note: This can prepared up to 3 days ahead, omitting the ice and club soda. Cover and chill. Pour over ice in highball glasses to 1/2 to 2/3 full. Top with club soda and garnish as above.*

Refreshing and "cool as a cucumber."

SERVES 6 TO 8

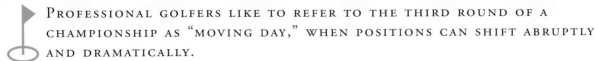

PROFESSIONAL GOLFERS LIKE TO REFER TO THE THIRD ROUND OF A CHAMPIONSHIP AS "MOVING DAY," WHEN POSITIONS CAN SHIFT ABRUPTLY AND DRAMATICALLY.

Lentil and Lemon Soup

6 slices bacon
3 carrots, sliced
2 ribs celery, sliced
1 onion, chopped
1 teaspoon minced garlic
1 1/2 cups dried lentils, rinsed and
  drained

6 cups chicken stock
1 teaspoon grated lemon zest
1 bay leaf
1/2 teaspoon salt
1/2 cup chopped fresh parsley
1/4 cup lemon juice
1 teaspoon cumin

◆ Cook the bacon in a large saucepan over medium-high heat until crisp; drain on paper towels and crumble.

◆ Remove all but 2 tablespoons of the bacon drippings from the saucepan. Add the carrots, celery, onion and garlic to the reserved drippings. Sauté over medium heat for 5 minutes or until the onion is tender.

◆ Stir in the lentils, stock, lemon zest, bay leaf and salt. Bring to a boil. Reduce the heat to medium and cover. Simmer for 35 to 45 minutes or until the lentils are tender. Remove the bay leaf and discard. Stir in the crumbled bacon, parsley, lemon juice and cumin.

A hearty soup with the freshness of lemon.

SERVES 8

You Thought You Didn't Like Lamb Chops

6 to 8 thick lamb chops
  (about 2 pounds)
1/2 cup soy sauce
1/2 cup water
2 tablespoons vegetable oil

2 tablespoons lemon juice
1 tablespoon brown sugar
1 heaping teaspoon minced garlic
1 teaspoon coarsely ground pepper
Several dashes of Tabasco sauce

◆ Place the lamb chops in a large sealable plastic bag.

◆ Mix the soy sauce, water, oil, lemon juice, brown sugar, garlic, pepper and Tabasco sauce in a bowl. Pour over the lamb and seal the bag. Marinate in the refrigerator overnight.

◆ Remove the lamb chops and discard the marinade.

◆ Cook on a preheated grill for 4 to 5 minutes for medium-rare.

◆ Remove to a serving platter and let stand for 5 minutes before serving to seal in the juices.

*The name speaks for itself—five-minute preparation for an
unbeatable combination of flavors.*

SERVES 6 TO 8

MASTERS® CO-FOUNDER BOB JONES RETIRED FROM COMPETITIVE GOLF AT THE AGE OF TWENTY-EIGHT AFTER WINNING GOLF'S GRAND SLAM.

Greek Chicken

8 garlic cloves, crushed
2 tablespoons olive oil
1 teaspoon salt
1 teaspoon pepper
2 teaspoons dried oregano

4 teaspoons fresh lemon juice
16 to 20 kalamata olives, pitted and
  halved
4 ounces feta cheese, crumbled
8 boneless skinless chicken breasts

◆ Combine the garlic, olive oil, salt, pepper, oregano, lemon juice, olives and cheese in a shallow baking pan. Stir to mix well. Add the chicken and turn to coat. Cover and marinate in the refrigerator for 4 hours.
◆ Bake at 350 degrees for 45 minutes or until cooked through.

Kalamata olives impart an exotic flavor to this simple chicken entrée.

SERVES 8

Greek Salad

1 head green leaf lettuce, torn into
  bite-size pieces
2 large tomatoes, cut into strips
1/2 large cucumber, peeled and diced
4 ounces feta cheese, crumbled

1 cup pitted black olives
1/2 cup olive oil
1/4 cup red wine vinegar
3/4 teaspoon oregano, crushed
Salt and pepper to taste

◆ Combine the lettuce, tomatoes, cucumber, cheese and olives in a large bowl.
◆ Whisk the olive oil, vinegar and oregano in a small bowl. Season with salt and pepper. Pour over the salad and toss to coat.

SERVES 6 TO 8

Almond Raisin Rice

2 tablespoons vegetable oil
1/2 cup chopped onion
8 ounces fresh mushrooms, sliced
1/4 cup chopped green bell pepper
3/4 teaspoon salt
3/4 teaspoon curry powder
1/2 teaspoon turmeric
1 cup white or brown rice

1 cup sliced almonds
3/4 cup golden raisins
1 (14 1/2-ounce) can condensed
   chicken broth plus enough water to
   measure 2 cups
Chopped fresh parsley for garnish
Toasted sliced almonds for garnish

◆ Heat the oil in a skillet. Add the onion, mushrooms and bell pepper and sauté until the vegetables are tender. Stir in the salt, curry powder and turmeric. Add the rice and stir until well coated. Pour into to a 2-quart baking dish.

◆ Place the almonds in a microwave-safe dish. Microwave on High for 2 minutes or until lightly browned, stirring every 30 seconds. Add to the rice mixture.

◆ Stir in the raisins and chicken broth with water and cover. Microwave on High for 5 minutes; stir. Microwave on Medium for 15 minutes for white rice or 40 minutes for brown rice or until all the liquid is absorbed and the rice is tender. Garnish with chopped parsley and toasted almonds.

A visual delight! Turmeric is worth using for its rich color and flavor.

SERVES 6 TO 8

Artichoke Spinach Pinwheels

1 (10-ounce) package frozen chopped spinach, thawed and drained well
1 (14-ounce) can artichoke hearts, drained and coarsely chopped
1/2 cup mayonnaise
1/2 cup grated Parmesan cheese
1 teaspoon onion powder
1 teaspoon garlic powder
1/2 teaspoon pepper
2 sheets frozen puff pastry, thawed for 30 minutes

◆ Combine the spinach, artichoke hearts, mayonnaise, cheese, onion powder, garlic powder and pepper in a bowl. Stir to mix well.
◆ Lay the puff pastry sheets on a work surface lightly dusted with flour. Spread the spinach mixture on the pastry sheets, leaving a 1/2-inch border. Roll up lengthwise. Place on a freezerproof plate and freeze for 20 minutes.
◆ Preheat the oven to 400 degrees.
◆ Cut the rolls into 1/2-inch slices. Arrange on a greased baking sheet. Bake for 20 minutes or until golden brown. Serve immediately.

SERVES 20 TO 24

JACK NICKLAUS, NICK FALDO, AND TIGER WOODS REMAIN THE ONLY PLAYERS TO HAVE WON THE MASTERS® IN CONSECUTIVE YEARS.

Citrus Trifle

1 large orange	3 cups heavy whipping cream,
16 ounces cream cheese, softened	whipped
2 cups confectioners' sugar	2 (3-ounce) packages sponge-style
Juice of 2 lemons	ladyfingers, split
2 teaspoons lemon extract	1 1/2 pints whole strawberries

◆ Grate the zest from the orange. Remove 1 teaspoon of grated zest and set aside. Juice the orange into a small bowl. Combine the remaining orange zest, cream cheese, confectioners' sugar, lemon juice and lemon extract in a large bowl. Beat with an electric mixer at low speed until smooth. Fold in the whipped cream.

◆ Brush the cut side of each split ladyfinger with orange juice. Line the bottom and halfway up the side of a trifle bowl or soufflé dish with half the ladyfingers, cut side in. Spoon half the cream cheese mixture into the bowl. Arrange the remaining ladyfingers around the inside of the bowl, overlapping if necessary. Spoon the remaining cream cheese mixture into the bowl.

◆ Place 1 whole strawberry in the center of the trifle. Split the remaining strawberries in half lengthwise. Arrange half the strawberries, cut side down, around the outside edge of the bowl. Arrange the remaining strawberries, cut side up, in a circular pattern between the outside strawberries and the center. Sprinkle with the reserved orange zest. Cover and chill for at least 2 hours to blend the flavors.

A light and refreshing dessert for company, with a striking presentation.

SERVES 16

Fall Fireside Supper

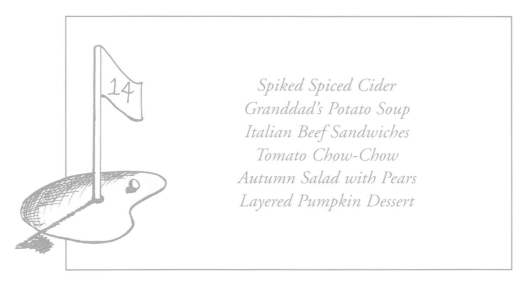

Spiked Spiced Cider
Granddad's Potato Soup
Italian Beef Sandwiches
Tomato Chow-Chow
Autumn Salad with Pears
Layered Pumpkin Dessert

The warmth of a fireplace and a menu reflecting simple tastes were features important to co-founder Clifford Roberts during the years he presided at the Augusta National Golf Club. Many friendships were fostered on the golf course, around the bridge table, and at the dinner table.

One of the most famous friendships that developed through the years at Augusta National was between Roberts and President Dwight D. Eisenhower. General Ike and his wife, Mamie, first visited the Augusta National Golf Club in 1948, and it was their first destination immediately after Ike's election to the presidency in 1952. The Eisenhower cabin was built by the Club in 1953 to accommodate the needs of the president during his visits and is one of ten cabins still used for lodging by members and guests.

This hearty, inviting menu will warm and satisfy family and friends during a season of packed school schedules and sporting events. After a long day spent in the crisp outdoors, you don't have to have a reason to invite the neighbors to "come on in" for a comfortable evening or a family game night.

Plan ahead for friends to join your family after a visit to the pumpkin patch, hayride, or football game. They will thank you for the relaxing break from the restaurant rush. There's no need to fuss with appetizers—warm up with mugs of Spiked Spiced Cider before you ladle out the soup and assemble the sandwiches. Simple and delicious, our soup and sandwich menu includes the tangy accompaniment Tomato Chow-Chow and the vivid flavors of an autumn salad.

Spiked Spiced Cider

1 (64-ounce) bottle apple cider
1 cup cranberry juice cocktail
1/2 teaspoon ground cinnamon
1/4 teaspoon ground allspice

1/4 teaspoon nutmeg
1 small orange, quartered
1 cup spiced rum (optional)

◆ Stir the cider, cranberry juice cocktail, cinnamon, allspice, nutmeg, orange and rum in a large saucepan. Heat to boiling. Reduce the heat and serve hot.

SERVES 10

Granddad's Potato Soup

5 large red-skinned potatoes, peeled
   and thinly sliced
4 (10-ounce) cans (or more) chicken
   broth
Salt and pepper to taste

2 cups half-and-half
1/2 cup (1 stick) butter
2 bunches green onions, sliced
1/4 white onion, finely chopped
2 ribs celery, finely chopped

◆ Combine the potatoes and broth in a 4-quart stockpot. Bring to a boil. Reduce the heat and cook for 15 minutes or until the potatoes are tender.
◆ Mash the potatoes with a wooden spoon. Season with salt and pepper. Stir in the half-and-half. Melt the butter in a skillet. Add the green onions, white onion and celery. Sauté until the vegetables are tender. Add to the soup and stir to mix well. Add more broth if the soup is too thick.

Your family will ask for this rich, creamy soup again and again.

SERVES 6 TO 8

Italian Beef Sandwiches

2 teaspoons dried basil
1 teaspoon dried oregano
1/2 teaspoon ground red pepper
1 (1-ounce) envelope dried onion
  soup mix

1 (3- to 4-pound) lean beef roast
1 package oblong French bread rolls,
  such as hoagies
1 (8-ounce) jar pepperoncini, drained
  (optional)

◆ Mix the basil, oregano, red pepper and soup mix in a small bowl. Rub into all sides of the roast. Place in a roasting pan and cover. Bake at 325 degrees for 4 hours. Remove the roast to a platter. Cover and chill. Place the pan with liquid in the refrigerator and chill until cold. Skim the fat. Remove the roasting juices to a saucepan and heat until hot. Cut the beef into very thin slices. Dip the insides of the rolls into the hot au jus and fill with sliced beef. Top with pepperoncini or Tomato Chow-Chow (page 128).

This can also be prepared in a slow cooker by adding one cup water and cooking on low for six to nine hours or until fork-tender.

SERVES 8

Tomato Chow-Chow

1¹/₂ teaspoons olive oil
2 tablespoons fresh ginger, minced
1¹/₂ teaspoons minced garlic
2 tablespoons fresh lemon juice
1 cinnamon stick
3 tomatoes, peeled, seeded and diced

2¹/₂ tablespoons brown sugar
¹/₄ teaspoon cumin
¹/₈ teaspoon crushed red pepper
1 tablespoon honey
Salt and pepper to taste

◆ Heat the olive oil in a saucepan. Add the ginger and garlic and sauté until the garlic is tender. Stir in the lemon juice and cinnamon stick. Reduce the heat and simmer until the liquid is slightly reduced. Stir in the tomatoes, brown sugar, cumin and crushed red pepper. Simmer until thick, stirring occasionally. Remove from the heat and stir in the honey. Remove the cinnamon stick. Season with salt and pepper.

Also great with corn bread.

SERVES 8

Autumn Salad with Pears

1 head romaine lettuce, torn
4 ounces bleu cheese or feta cheese,
    crumbled
1 (8-ounce) can water chestnuts,
    drained and chopped

2 onions, finely chopped
4 pears
Lemon juice
³/₄ cup coarsely chopped pecans
1 bottle balsamic vinaigrette

◆ Combine the romaine, cheese, water chestnuts and onions in a large bowl. Toss well to mix. Core and slice the pears. Sprinkle with lemon juice. Add to the salad and toss gently. Sprinkle with the pecans. Sprinkle lightly with vinaigrette and serve immediately.

SERVES 6 TO 8

Layered Pumpkin Dessert

First Layer
1 (2-layer) package yellow
   cake mix
1/2 cup (1 stick) margarine,
   melted
1 egg, beaten

Second Layer
1 1/2 (15-ounce) cans
   pumpkin
3 eggs, beaten
1/2 cup packed brown sugar
1/2 cup granulated sugar
2/3 cup evaporated milk
1/2 teaspoon ground
   cinnamon

Third Layer
1/2 cup granulated sugar
1/2 teaspoon ground
   cinnamon
1/2 cup (1 stick) margarine
Vanilla ice cream

◆ *For the first layer,* remove 1 cup of the cake mix to a bowl and set aside. Combine the remaining cake mix, melted margarine and egg in a bowl. Stir to mix well. Press onto the bottom of a greased 9×13-inch baking pan.

◆ *For the second layer,* beat the pumpkin, eggs, brown sugar, granulated sugar, evaporated milk and cinnamon in a bowl. Spread over the first layer in the baking pan.

◆ *For the third layer,* preheat the oven to 350 degrees. Stir the granulated sugar and cinnamon into the reserved cake mix. Cut in the margarine with a pastry blender or fork until crumbly. Sprinkle over the 2nd layer. Bake for 60 to 70 minutes. Serve warm with vanilla ice cream or cool and cut into bars.

SERVES 20

"WINNING THE 1937 MASTERS® MADE A HUGE CONTRIBUTION TO MY GOLF GAME. IT CONVINCED ME I WAS A GOOD PLAYER. I KNEW IN MY HEART I COULD WIN, AND FROM THAT POINT FORWARD NOTHING MUCH SCARED ME ON THE GOLF COURSE."

—BYRON NELSON, TWO-TIME MASTERS® CHAMPION (1937, 1942)

Holiday Dessert Buffet

Almond Toffee
Coconut Balls
Peppermint Whip in Chocolate Bag
Lemon Bites
Grand Marnier Mousse Cake
Five-Star Fruit Tart
Red Velvet Cake
Coffee Bar
Champagne Cocktails

A Holiday Dessert Buffet is a festive way to celebrate friendships during the giving season. Hold a solo Open House, or plan to have several hostesses share in the preparation. Invite companions from work, church, and school to mingle. A dessert party is also a sumptuous way to bring friends together after attending a performance of the Nutcracker ballet or a holiday concert.

Whether you decide to dress up your dining room table or serve from a cozy kitchen, it is especially nice during this busy season to prepare your table the week ahead. Match your serving pieces to menu items early, and have fun combining seasonal designs with bright metals and solids. To construct your own tiered platter, place a dessert compote or a pretty glass between a dinner plate and a salad plate.

Accent the table the day of your event with seasonal foliage—Southern favorites often found at home are holly sprigs and magnolia leaves and blooms. Fresh fruit or jeweled ornaments also work beautifully, and candles always add a finishing touch. Choose the drama of a candelabra in the dining room or welcoming tea lights in the kitchen.

Our menu features the irresistible combination of chocolate and fruit—it's always nice to have something lemony to balance the sweetness. A cookie swirled in Peppermint Whip, served in the show-stopping, edible Chocolate Bag, is a special presentation worthy of the holidays.

Elegant Champagne Cocktails or a selection from a Coffee Bar will satisfy most guests. Offer fanciful topping choices such as whipped cream, cinnamon, chocolate sprinkles, cocoa, and assorted flavored liqueurs.

Almond Toffee

1 cup (2 sticks) butter, chilled
1 cup sugar
1 (7-ounce) chocolate candy bar

1 cup toasted almonds, coarsely chopped

◆ Combine the cold butter and sugar in a heavy saucepan. Cook over high heat to a deep amber color, stirring constantly with a wooden spoon. Pour immediately into a foil-lined 9×13-inch baking pan and spread evenly. Let cool until hardened.
◆ Melt half the chocolate in a small saucepan over very low heat. Spread over the toffee. Sprinkle with half the almonds. Let cool. Invert the toffee onto a work surface and remove the foil.
◆ Melt the remaining chocolate in a small saucepan over very low heat. Spread over the uncoated side of the toffee. Sprinkle with the remaining almonds. Break into pieces when cool.

*A sought-after local recipe, sure to be appreciated at your table
or as a special holiday gift.*

SERVES 24

"THE TEE SHOT HERE IS BY FAR THE SCARIEST SHOT ON THE COURSE. IN FACT, YOU OFTEN SEE PLAYERS PULL OUT ONE CLUB AND THEN PUT IT BACK IN THE BAG."

—BERNHARD LANGER, TWO-TIME MASTERS® CHAMPION (1985, 1993)
DESCRIBING PAR 3 HOLE NUMBER 12, GOLDEN BELL

Coconut Balls

1 (2-pound) package confectioners' sugar
1/2 cup (1 stick) butter, softened
1 (14-ounce) can sweetened condensed milk

1 teaspoon vanilla extract
1 (14-ounce) package flaked coconut
4 cups semisweet chocolate chips
1/4 cup shortening

◆ Combine the confectioners' sugar, butter, sweetened condensed milk, vanilla and coconut in a large bowl. Stir to mix well. Shape teaspoonfuls of the mixture into balls (you may wish to butter your hands). Place the coconut balls on a waxed paper-lined or nonstick baking sheet. Place in the refrigerator or freezer and chill until firm.

◆ Combine the chocolate chips and shortening in a microwave-safe bowl. Microwave on High until melted, stirring occasionally. Working with a few coconut balls at a time, skewer one with a wooden pick, then dip into melted chocolate. Return to waxed paper or place on a marble candy slab to firm up.

◆ *Note: Like many candies, these taste better after they "cure" for a day or two (if they last that long!).*

For a pretty gift-giving idea, place each candy in a small paper confectionery cup while still warm. Or, once candies cool, wrap them individually in specialty candy wrappers, which are available at some specialty baking stores.

MAKES 5 DOZEN COCONUT BALLS

Peppermint Whip

2 (7-ounce) bags peppermint candies, unwrapped	2/3 cup confectioners' sugar
3 cups heavy whipping cream	Pirouette or shortbread cookies or Chocolate Bag (page 135)

◆ Place the candies in a sealable plastic bag. Crush with the back of a spoon or a meat mallet.

◆ Whip the cream in a bowl. Beat in the confectioners' sugar until blended. Fold in the crushed candy. Cover and chill for several hours for the colors to blend.

◆ Serve with cookies or in a Chocolate Bag.

Looks and tastes like Christmas!

SERVES 25

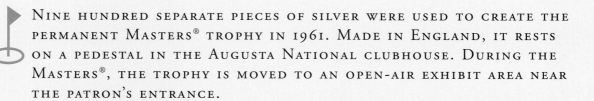

NINE HUNDRED SEPARATE PIECES OF SILVER WERE USED TO CREATE THE PERMANENT MASTERS® TROPHY IN 1961. MADE IN ENGLAND, IT RESTS ON A PEDESTAL IN THE AUGUSTA NATIONAL CLUBHOUSE. DURING THE MASTERS®, THE TROPHY IS MOVED TO AN OPEN-AIR EXHIBIT AREA NEAR THE PATRON'S ENTRANCE.

Chocolate Bag

1 (3×5×11-inch) nonrecycled paper lunch bag | 4 cups semisweet chocolate chips

◆ Cut 4 inches off the top of the bag to make it 7 inches in length. Stuff a plastic grocery bag in the bottom of the paper bag to hold its shape and keep the bottom flat and corners square. Invert the bag onto a 1-liter bottle or other form to hold it in place.

◆ Melt the chocolate chips in the top of a double boiler over simmering water, stirring until smooth. Coat the paper bag liberally with nonstick cooking spray. Dip a pastry brush in the melted chocolate and begin painting the bag with chocolate. Continue until no paper is visible. Chill the bag on its holder overnight to harden.

◆ Melt the remaining chocolate again over simmering water. Paint the bag with a second coat of chocolate. Chill the bag on its holder until hardened. Repeat with another coat of chocolate if the coating does not appear thick enough to remove the bag without breaking the coating.

◆ Remove the bag from the hardened chocolate coating by carefully sliding the tip of a thin sharp knife between the top of the bag and the coating. Work the knife gently around the entire edge to separate. Pull out the paper bag and lay the chocolate bag on its side on a serving plate.

The fun is to break the bag and dip. You will have to be first because your guests will think it is too pretty to mess up.

MAKES 1 BAG

Lemon Bites

Shells

1 cup all-purpose flour
1/2 cup finely chopped pecans
1/4 cup sugar
1 egg
1/4 cup (1/2 stick) butter, softened

Filling

1 teaspoon unflavored gelatin
1 tablespoon cold water

2 eggs
1/2 cup sugar
2 tablespoons grated lemon zest
1/4 cup fresh lemon juice
2 tablespoons butter
Whipped cream and additional grated
  lemon zest for garnish

◆ *For the shells,* preheat the oven to 375 degrees. Mix the flour, pecans and sugar in a bowl. Add the egg and butter and mix until crumbly. Press the dough onto the bottoms and sides of ungreased miniature muffin cups. Bake for 10 to 12 minutes or until light golden brown. Remove the pans to a wire rack to cool.

◆ *For the filling,* soften the gelatin in the cold water in a saucepan. Beat the eggs and sugar in a bowl. Stir into the gelatin mixture. Bring to a boil, stirring constantly. Reduce the heat and simmer for 10 minutes. Remove from the heat and stir in the lemon zest, lemon juice and butter. Pour the filling into the baked shells. Chill for 1 hour or until set. Remove from the muffin cups to a serving platter. Garnish with whipped cream and grated lemon zest.

The shells can be made a few days in advance and stored in an airtight container.

SERVES 24

SPAIN'S SEVE BALLESTEROS BECAME THE THEN-YOUNGEST MASTERS® CHAMPION IN 1980, AS WELL AS THE FIRST EUROPEAN TO WIN THE TITLE.

Grand Marnier Mousse Cake

2 cups minus 1 tablespoon sifted
  cake flour
$1/4$ teaspoon plus $1/8$ teaspoon
  baking powder
$3/4$ teaspoon baking soda
$1/2$ teaspoon salt
$3/4$ cup sifted baking cocoa
1 cup hot water

2 eggs
$1^1/4$ cups sugar
$3/4$ cup vegetable oil
10 ounces white chocolate
3 cups heavy whipping cream
2 tablespoons Grand Marnier
Fresh strawberries or raspberries
  for garnish

◆ Preheat the oven to 350 degrees.

◆ Mix the flour, baking powder, baking soda and salt in a bowl. Combine the baking cocoa and hot water in a bowl. Stir to mix well. Beat the eggs and sugar in a bowl with an electric mixer at low speed. Beat in the oil gradually. Beat in the dry ingredients alternately with the cocoa mixture. Pour into 2 greased and floured 9-inch cake pans. Bake for 25 to 30 minutes or until a wooden pick inserted in the center comes out clean. Cool in the pans for 10 minutes. Remove to a wire rack to cool completely.

◆ Cut 1 layer into 1-inch cubes and set aside. Place the other layer in the bottom of a 9-inch springform pan. Melt the white chocolate in the top of a double boiler over simmering water, stirring until smooth. Whip the cream in a bowl until soft peaks form. Stir in the Grand Marnier. Fold in the melted chocolate quickly. Fold in the cake cubes. Spread over the cake layer in the springform pan. Cover and chill for at least 3 hours and up to 24 hours. Loosen from the side of the pan with a sharp knife and remove the side. Place on a serving plate and garnish with strawberries or raspberries.

—CADWALLADERS CAFÉ

Spoil your guests with this lavish dessert.

SERVES 12

Five-Star Fruit Tart

Crust
1 1/3 cups gingersnap
  crumbs
2/3 cup vanilla wafer
  crumbs
3 tablespoons sugar
6 tablespoons unsalted
  butter, melted

Filling
16 ounces cream cheese,
  softened
6 tablespoons sugar
3 tablespoons amaretto
2 teaspoons vanilla extract
2 teaspoons almond extract

Topping
1 1/2 pints blueberries
1 1/2 pints raspberries
3 or 4 kiwifruit, peeled and
  thinly sliced
1/4 cup apricot preserves
1 tablespoon amaretto

◆ *For the crust,* mix the gingersnap crumbs, vanilla wafer crumbs, sugar and melted butter in a bowl. Press onto the bottom and up the side of a tart pan; chill.

◆ *For the filling,* beat the cream cheese and sugar in a bowl until light and fluffy. Add the amaretto, vanilla and almond extract. Beat until smooth. Spread over the prepared crust. Cover and chill until firm or up to 24 hours ahead.

◆ *For the topping,* arrange the blueberries, raspberries and kiwifruit on top of the filling. Melt the preserves in a small saucepan over low heat. Stir in the amaretto. Brush over the fruit. Cover and chill for up to 2 hours. Cut into wedges and serve.

A testing committee favorite! Gingersnap cookie crust and accents of almond make this an extraordinary fruit tart.

SERVES 12

"THE "MASTERS" HAS A SPECIAL PLACE AND TIME IN MY LIFE. THERE ARE SUCH GREAT MEMORIES, AND MEMORIES ARE THE CUSHION OF LIFE."

—GARY PLAYER, THREE-TIME MASTERS CHAMPION (1961, 1974, 1978)

Red Velvet Cake

Cake

2^1/$_2$ cups all-purpose flour
1 tablespoon baking soda
1 tablespoon baking cocoa
1^1/$_2$ cups sugar
2 eggs
1^1/$_2$ cups vegetable oil
1 tablespoon vanilla extract
1 tablespoon vinegar

1 tablespoon red food coloring
1 cup buttermilk

Frosting

^{1}/$_2$ cup (1 stick) butter, softened
8 ounces cream cheese, softened
1 teaspoon vanilla extract
1 (1-pound) package confectioners'
   sugar

◆ *For the cake,* preheat the oven to 350 degrees. Sift the flour, baking soda and baking cocoa together. Beat the sugar, eggs, oil, vanilla, vinegar and food coloring in a bowl. Stir in the dry ingredients alternately with the buttermilk. Pour into 3 greased and floured 8-inch cake pans. Bake for 15 to 20 minutes or until a wooden pick inserted in the center comes out clean. Cool in the pans for 10 minutes. Remove to a wire rack to cool completely.

◆ *For the frosting,* beat the butter, cream cheese, vanilla and confectioners' sugar in a bowl until smooth. Spread between the layers and over the top and side of the cake.

—BARBARA NICKLAUS, WIFE OF JACK NICKLAUS

SERVES 12

Coffee Bar

1 gallon water

8 ounces coffee

Sweeteners: Rock sugar, Turbinado sugar, granulated sugar

Creamers: Half-and-half or light cream, flavored creamers

Flavored syrups: Irish mist, vanilla, hazelnut

Liqueurs: Drambuie, B and B, Bailey's Irish Cream, Chambord, Grand Marnier, Amaretto, Kahlúa

Toppings: Ground cardamom, ground cinnamon, grated orange zest, cocoa, cinnamon sticks

Whipped cream

Nice extras:
Rocksugar stirrers
Chocolate spoons

◆ Arrange the coffee cups next to the coffee pots. Next to them, place the sweeteners in little bowls or ramekins—a three-compartment dip or dressing caddy is ideal. Pour the creamers into cream pitchers or other decorative containers, but leave the syrups in bottles—they're attractive on a buffet and guests can distinguish between varieties.

◆ Next arrange the liqueurs in an attractive grouping.

◆ Place the whipped cream in a silver, crystal, or other pretty bowl with a spoon or two. The toppings go next-to-last in the spread, in either shakers or salt cellars with tiny spoons. Use silver cups to hold chocolate spoons and rock sugar stirrers. Offer saucers or napkins.

MAKES ENOUGH COFFEE FOR 16

Champagne Cocktails

6 sugar cubes	6 maraschino cherries
12 dashes angostura bitters	1 (750-milliliter) bottle Champagne

◆ Place 1 sugar cube in each of 6 Champagne flutes.
◆ Top each cube with 2 dashes of bitters and 1 cherry.
◆ Fill glasses with Champagne.

Enhanced Champagne for a sweet celebration.

SERVES 6

ALISTER MACKENZIE, SERVING IN SOUTH AFRICA AS A CIVIL SURGEON IN THE BRITISH ARMY, BECAME SO FASCINATED WITH CAMOUFLAGE TECHNIQUES THAT HE APPLIED THEM A FEW YEARS LATER TO HIS NEW CAREER IN GOLF COURSE DESIGN—A CAREER THAT INCLUDED WORKING ALONGSIDE BOB JONES IN THE CREATION OF AUGUSTA NATIONAL GOLF CLUB.

Festive Family Christmas Eve

Cranberry Chutney
Hot Bacon and Swiss Spread
Shrimp and Grits
Balsamic Bermuda Onion Salad
Foolproof Homemade Yeast Rolls
Mochaccino Cake
Hotty-Toddy Toaster

Wrapping . . . baking . . . caroling . . . dancing . . . talking . . . playing . . . praying . . . greeting . . . cooking . . . toasting . . . and wrapping some more!

It's that final day of anticipation, with so many special things to do—neighborhood visits, worship, and, of course, duties as Santa's helper. The customs of each family may vary, but all families cherish the time spent together.

You can wrap up your holiday preparations and have a festive and memorable family dinner, too. In this Christmas Eve menu, we have given attention to our fondness for favorite things, such as warm rolls to pass around the table, comforting creamy grits with spicy shrimp, a spectacular salad, and a luscious cake combining coffee and chocolate.

The homemade yeast rolls are "foolproof," which is essential on a night as busy as Christmas Eve. The main dish is a splurge certain to please your family and can wait on the stove until you are ready to serve.

From preparation to celebration, care has been taken to plan a meal that is not too heavy or labor intensive. We all know there is plenty to do later in the evening!

Cranberry Chutney

2 cups fresh cranberries
1/2 cup water
1/2 cup raisins
1 small onion, chopped
1 scant cup sugar
1/4 teaspoon ground cinnamon
1/4 teaspoon ginger

1/8 teaspoon each allspice and salt
1 (8-ounce) can crushed pineapple
1/4 cup chopped celery
1/4 cup chopped pecans or walnuts
1/2 cup chopped cored peeled apple
1 to 2 tablespoon lemon juice
8 ounces block-style cream cheese

✦ Combine the cranberries, water, raisins, onion, sugar, cinnamon, ginger, allspice and salt in a heavy saucepan. Cook over medium heat for 15 minutes or until the cranberries pop, stirring occasionally. Stir in the pineapple, celery, pecans, apple and lemon juice. Cook over low heat for 30 minutes, stirring frequently. Serve warm or chilled over the cream cheese on a serving plate.

—FROM *Second Round Tea-Time at the* MASTERS®

MAKES 3 1/2 CUPS

Hot Bacon and Swiss Spread

8 ounces cream cheese, softened
1/2 cup mayonnaise
1 cup (4 ounces) shredded Swiss
    cheese

2 tablespoons chopped green onions
8 slices bacon, crisp-cooked and
    crumbled
Butter crackers

✦ Preheat the oven to 350 degrees. Combine the cream cheese, mayonnaise, Swiss cheese and green onions in a bowl. Stir to mix well. Spoon into a baking dish. Top with the bacon. Bake for 15 to 20 minutes. Serve with butter crackers.

SERVES 10

Shrimp and Grits

2 to 2¹/2 pounds deveined peeled
  medium shrimp
6 tablespoons lemon juice
Cayenne pepper to taste
8 cups chicken broth
2 cups white grits
1 cup half-and-half
Salt and pepper to taste

7 slices bacon, coarsely chopped
2 onions, diced
4 garlic cloves, minced
1 large red bell pepper, diced
2 (28-ounce) cans diced tomatoes
¹/4 cup cocktail sauce
¹/2 teaspoon salt
¹/8 teaspoon pepper

◆ Sprinkle the shrimp with the lemon juice and season with cayenne pepper. Set aside.

◆ Bring the broth to a boil in a large heavy saucepan. Stir in the grits slowly and reduce the heat to low. Cook for 25 to 30 minutes or until the grits are softened and thick, stirring frequently. Stir in the half-and-half. Cook for 10 minutes, stirring occasionally. Season with salt and pepper. Remove from the heat and keep warm. Add more chicken broth or water if the grits become too thick.

◆ Cook the bacon in a large skillet until crisp; drain on paper towels and crumble. Remove all but 3 tablespoons of the bacon drippings from the skillet. Add the onions and garlic and sauté for 5 to 7 minutes. Add the bell pepper and sauté for 7 to 9 minutes or until the vegetables are tender. Stir in the tomatoes, cocktail sauce, ¹/2 teaspoon salt and ¹/8 teaspoon pepper. Simmer for 1 hour, stirring occasionally. Stir in the shrimp and cook for 5 minutes or until the shrimp turn pink. Serve over the grits and top with the bacon.

◆ *Note: Increase the heat by adding more cocktail sauce or jalapeño chiles.*

SERVES 8

Balsamic Bermuda Onion Salad

Onions

1/4 cup olive oil
1/4 cup balsamic vinegar
1 teaspoon kosher salt
1/2 teaspoon pepper
3 small red onions, cut into
   rings
2 tablespoons balsamic vinegar

Salad

6 tablespoons minced shallots
2 teaspoons Dijon mustard
1/4 cup red wine vinegar
1/2 teaspoon kosher salt
1/2 teaspoon pepper
3/4 cup olive oil
2 heads red leaf lettuce, torn

◆ *For the onions,* preheat the oven to 375 degrees. Whisk the olive oil, 1/4 cup balsamic vinegar, salt and pepper in a bowl. Add the onion rings and toss to coat. Spoon into a baking dish. Bake for 15 minutes. Sprinkle with 2 tablespoons balsamic vinegar; let cool.

◆ *For the salad,* whisk the shallots, Dijon mustard, red wine vinegar, salt and pepper in a large bowl. Whisk in the olive oil slowly. Add the lettuce just before serving and toss to coat. Arrange the salad on salad plates and top with the onion rings.

This simple plated salad will dress up any occasion.

SERVES 10 TO 12

Foolproof Homemade Yeast Rolls

1 cup shortening
1 cup sugar
1 tablespoon salt
1 cup boiling water

2 envelopes dry yeast
1 cup warm water
4 eggs, beaten
6 cups all-purpose flour

◆ Combine the shortening, sugar and salt in a large bowl. Add the boiling water and stir until the shortening melts. Let cool to lukewarm.

◆ Dissolve the yeast in the warm water in a small bowl and let stand for 5 minutes or until the yeast slightly foams. Add the dissolved yeast and eggs to the shortening mixture and stir to mix well. Stir in the flour, 1 cup at a time, to make a stiff dough. Cover and chill for at least 12 hours.

◆ Remove the dough from the refrigerator 3 hours before baking. Knead the dough a few times on a well-floured work surface. Roll out the dough and cut with a 2-inch biscuit cutter. Arrange the rolls in a greased baking pan. Let rise in a warm place for 3 hours.

◆ Preheat the oven to 400 degrees. Bake for 12 to 15 minutes or until golden brown.

This versatile dough can be made into loaves or individual rolls.
It can also be baked and frozen until needed.

MAKES 2 DOZEN ROLLS

Mochaccino Cake

1 (2-layer) package devil's food
  cake mix
3 eggs
1 cup water
1/2 cup heavy whipping cream
1/4 cup vegetable oil

2 tablespoons baking cocoa
2 tablespoons instant coffee powder
1 cup miniature chocolate chips
2 tablespoons heavy whipping cream
2 tablespoons instant coffee powder
2 (16-ounce) containers vanilla frosting

◆ Preheat the oven to 350 degrees. Combine the cake mix, eggs, water, 1/2 cup heavy cream, oil, baking cocoa and 2 tablespoons coffee powder in a bowl. Beat with an electric mixer at low speed until blended. Beat at medium speed for 2 minutes. Stir in the chocolate chips. Pour into 2 greased and floured 9-inch cake pans.

◆ Bake for 25 to 30 minutes or until a wooden pick inserted in the center comes out clean. Cool in the pans for 20 minutes. Remove to a wire rack to cool completely.

◆ Mix 2 tablespoons heavy cream and 2 tablespoons coffee powder in a bowl. Add the vanilla frosting and stir to mix well. Spread between the layers and over the top and side of the cake.

Chocolate and coffee all wrapped up in one scrumptious layer cake.

SERVES 12

Hotty-Toddy Toaster

3/4 ounce Tuaca (an Italian liqueur) Hot coffee
3/4 ounce Kahlúa Whipped cream
1/4 ounce Bailey's Irish cream liqueur Chocolate shavings (optional)

✦ Combine the Tuaca, Kahlúa and Bailey's Irish cream in a large mug. Fill with hot coffee and stir.

✦ Top with whipped cream and chocolate shavings.

SERVES I

WE ALWAYS ENJOY COMING TO AUGUSTA FOR A FEW REASONS. THE GOLF FANS ARE VERY SAVVY AND MORE THAN AT ANY OTHER EVENT THEY KNOW AND APPRECIATE A TRULY GOOD SHOT. IT'S SO MUCH A PART OF THE MASTERS FOR US TO SEE SO MANY OF THE SAME PEOPLE EACH YEAR, OFTEN IN THE SAME PLACES ON THE COURSE, FROM MARSHALS TO THE AUGUSTA NATIONAL MEMBERS. OUR FAMILY STAYS NEAR THE COURSE IN A WONDERFUL AREA WHERE OUR HOSTS AND NEIGHBORS ALWAYS ARE SO RESPECTFUL AND SUPPORTIVE. AND OF COURSE WE LOVE THE SOUTHERN DISHES OUR CHEF LIKES TO PREPARE WHEN HE'S IN GEORGIA. THAT OLD "SOUTHERN HOSPITALITY" IS ABSOLUTELY NOT JUST A CLICHÉ FOR US. WE CAN'T WAIT TO COME BACK TO THE MASTERS AGAIN AND AGAIN.

—AMY MICKELSON, WIFE OF PHIL MICKELSON, MASTERS® CHAMPION (2004)

Gathering for the Augusta Futurity, A Down-Home Barbecue

Jalapeño Black-Eyed Pea Dip
Apple Dip
Boiled Peanuts
Slow-Cooker Barbecue
Ribs with Honey Barbecue Sauce
Five-Vegetable Slaw
Curried Kidney Beans
Crustless Corn Pie
Sour Cream Biscuits or Buns
Cinnamon Walnut Bread Pudding with Whiskey Sauce

Whether you are hosting cowboys or city boys, a barbecue is sure to satisfy. We've taken the guesswork out of sought-after Southern favorites and left in all of the flavor!

Each January, Augusta plays host to the finest cutting horses and riders in the country at the Augusta Futurity, the largest cutting-horse competition east of the Mississippi. Born from the need to separate, or cut, cattle from the herd, cutting is a sport that showcases the horses' skills in handling cattle. Riders have celebrated this heritage through competition at the Augusta Futurity since 1979.

Our barbecue menu is full of hearty Southern tradition, but without the traditional hours of preparation needed for that "secret recipe" tangy, rich flavor. Slow-Cooker Barbecue fits into any timetable, and, after a start in the oven, the Ribs with Honey Barbecue Sauce only require minimal grilling time.

Add flair to a cool-weather tailgate with an ample selection of appetizers and side dishes. Apple Dip is delightfully sweet with crisp fall apples and is a snap to mix, and our unique and tasty versions of slaw, beans, and corn just may become your new classics.

Visitors to the South remember sampling boiled peanuts—many Southerners have purchased their boiled peanuts from the same roadside vendor for years. With our recipe, you can have them made to your own liking anytime!

Jalapeño Black-Eyed Pea Dip

3 (16-ounce) cans black-eyed peas
1/2 cup chopped onion
3 canned jalapeño chiles, seeded and
    chopped
1 teaspoon jalapeño juice
1 garlic clove, minced

1 (4-ounce) can chopped green chiles
1/2 cup (1 stick) butter
2 cups (8 ounces) sharp Cheddar
    cheese, shredded, plus additional for
    topping
Tortilla chips

◆ Preheat the oven to 350 degrees. Rinse and drain 2 cans of the peas. Process the peas, onion, jalapeños, juice, garlic and green chiles in a food processor fitted with a steel blade. Remove to a bowl. Rinse and drain the remaining can of peas and stir into the processed pea mixture.

◆ Combine the butter and 8 ounces Cheddar cheese in a saucepan. Cook over low heat until melted, stirring occasionally. Add to the black-eyed pea mixture and mix well. Pour into a baking dish. Top with additional Cheddar cheese.

◆ Bake for 20 minutes or until the cheese melts. Serve hot with tortilla chips.

Bring "good luck" to your New Year's Day football
fare with this warm, cheesy dip.

SERVES 15

Apple Dip

8 ounces cream cheese, softened
1/2 cup packed brown sugar
1/2 cup granulated sugar
1 (10-ounce) package toffee bits

1/2 teaspoon vanilla extract
Red and green apple slices
Lemon juice

◆ Mix the cream cheese, brown sugar, granulated sugar, toffee bits and vanilla in a bowl. Cover and chill.
◆ Dip the apple slices in the lemon juice to prevent browning. Serve the dip surrounded by apple slices.

This is a good alternative to a fruit tray. The dip is sweet enough for a light dessert.

SERVES 8 TO 10

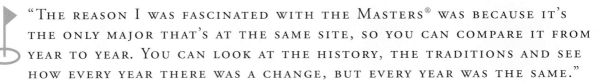

"THE REASON I WAS FASCINATED WITH THE MASTERS® WAS BECAUSE IT'S THE ONLY MAJOR THAT'S AT THE SAME SITE, SO YOU CAN COMPARE IT FROM YEAR TO YEAR. YOU CAN LOOK AT THE HISTORY, THE TRADITIONS AND SEE HOW EVERY YEAR THERE WAS A CHANGE, BUT EVERY YEAR WAS THE SAME."

—TIGER WOODS, FOUR-TIME MASTERS® CHAMPION (1997, 2001, 2002, 2005)

Boiled Peanuts

2 pounds green peanuts   3/4 cup salt

◆ Rinse the peanuts and drain. Discard any imperfect peanuts.
◆ Cover the peanuts with water in a large saucepan. Bring to a boil. Reduce the heat to low and simmer for at least 2 hours or until soft but not mushy.
◆ Remove from the heat and stir in the salt. Let stand for 45 minutes. Taste to determine saltiness. Taste every 15 minutes until desired saltiness is reached; drain.

When green peanuts are not in season, use dried raw peanuts, soaking overnight in water. Drain and cover with fresh water before boiling. These can also be cooked in a slow cooker for 8 to 10 hours.

SERVES 6 TO 8

Slow-Cooker Barbecue

1 (3- to 4-pound) bone-in pork loin   2 tablespoons sugar
   roast, trimmed   2 cups cider vinegar
1 tablespoon salt   1/4 to 1/2 cup ketchup
Pepper to taste   8 toasted hamburger buns

◆ Season the roast on all sides with the salt and pepper. Place the roast in a slow cooker. Sprinkle with the sugar and add the vinegar. Cover and cook on low for 8 to 10 hours or until the meat falls from the bones. Remove the roast to a work surface. Shred the meat with a fork, discarding the fat and bones. Place the meat in a bowl. Add just enough pan juices and ketchup to moisten the meat. Serve on the toasted buns.

Slow cooked in the kitchen instead of the barbecue pit!

SERVES 8

Ribs with Honey Barbecue Sauce

3 to 4 pounds baby back pork ribs
Salt and pepper to taste

Honey Barbecue Sauce (below)

◆ Rub the ribs with salt and pepper. Arrange in a large baking dish. Fill halfway with water. Cover with foil. Bake at 350 degrees for 1¹/2 hours. Turn the ribs over and cover with foil. Bake at 350 degrees for 1¹/2 hours. Turn off the oven and leave the ribs in the oven while making the Honey Barbecue Sauce. Remove the ribs and coat in the sauce. Place on a hot grill. Cook for 15 minutes, coating often with sauce, turning the ribs once.

If using pork spareribs or country-style ribs, increase the baking time by 30 minutes.

SERVES 6

Honey Barbecue Sauce

1 cup ketchup
1/2 cup water
1/4 cup cider vinegar
1 tablespoon brown sugar
3 tablespoons honey
2 tablespoons red pepper jelly
1 tablespoon Worcestershire sauce

1¹/2 teaspoons salt
1/2 teaspoon dry mustard
1 teaspoon chili powder
1¹/2 teaspoons liquid smoke
Dash of garlic powder
Dash of onion salt
Dash of lemon juice

◆ Mix the ketchup, water, cider vinegar, brown sugar, honey, jelly, Worcestershire sauce, salt, dry mustard, chili powder, liquid smoke, garlic powder, onion salt and lemon juice in a saucepan. Cook over low heat for 10 minutes, stirring occasionally.

A well-guarded prize-winning local recipe!

MAKES ABOUT 2 CUPS

Five-Vegetable Slaw

1 (16-ounce) package shredded
  cabbage
1 red bell pepper, cut into thin strips
1 green bell pepper, cut into thin
  strips
1/2 seedless cucumber, halved
  lengthwise and thinly sliced

4 scallions, thinly sliced diagonally
Juice of 2 limes
1/4 cup honey
3 tablespoons vegetable oil
Salt and pepper to taste

◆ Combine the cabbage, red bell pepper, green bell pepper, cucumber and scallions in a large bowl. Whisk the lime juice and honey in a small bowl. Whisk in the oil slowly.
◆ Pour over the vegetables and season with salt and pepper. Toss well to mix.

A super side dish that's also great served on a piled-high barbecue sandwich.

SERVES 6 TO 8

WITH THE GOAL TO CONTRIBUTE TO THE WAR EFFORT, OVER 200 HEAD OF CATTLE AND MORE THAN 1,000 TURKEYS GRAZED AUGUSTA NATIONAL'S FAIRWAYS IN 1943, WHILE THE CLUB WAS CLOSED DURING WORLD WAR II. TURKEYS WERE ALSO SENT TO MEMBERS AS GIFTS THAT YEAR, AND PECANS WERE HARVESTED FROM THE GROUNDS AND DONATED TO THE ARMY CANTEEN.

Curried Kidney Beans

2 onions, chopped
2 green bell peppers, chopped
2 tart apples, cored and chopped
2 teaspoons (or more) curry powder
1/2 cup (1 stick) butter, melted
2 (28-ounce) cans tomatoes

4 (15-ounce) cans kidney beans,
　drained
2 cups packed brown sugar
2 tablespoons white vinegar
Salt and freshly ground pepper to taste
Freshly grated Parmesan cheese

◆ Preheat the oven to 350 degrees. Sauté the onions, bell peppers, apples and curry powder in the butter in a skillet until tender. Drain the tomatoes and squeeze out all liquid. Combine the onion mixture, tomatoes, beans, brown sugar and vinegar in a bowl. Season with salt and pepper and mix well. Spoon into a baking dish. Bake for 30 minutes. Sprinkle with Parmesan cheese before serving.

An uncommon medley we promise you will love!

SERVES 12

Crustless Corn Pie

2/3 cup milk

2 eggs

1 tablespoon sugar

1 tablespoon all-purpose flour

Salt to taste

1 (20-ounce) roll frozen cream-style
    Silver Queen corn, thawed

2 tablespoons margarine, melted

◆ Preheat the oven to 350 degrees. Combine the milk, eggs, sugar and flour in a bowl. Season with salt. Stir to mix well. Stir in the corn and melted margarine. Pour into a greased 9×9-inch baking dish. Bake for 45 to 50 minutes or until golden brown.

SERVES 6

Sour Cream Biscuits

2 cups self-rising flour

1 cup (2 sticks) butter, softened

1 cup sour cream

◆ Preheat the oven to 350 degrees. Cut the flour and butter together with a pastry blender or fork until crumbly. Add the sour cream and stir just until moistened. Fill greased miniature muffin cups. Bake for 20 to 25 minutes or until golden brown.

MAKES 2 DOZEN BISCUITS

Cinnamon Walnut Bread Pudding with Whiskey Sauce

Pudding

1 loaf French bread, torn into
small pieces
4 cups milk
2 cups sugar
3 eggs
1 cup walnuts, chopped
2 tablespoons vanilla extract

1 1/2 teaspoons ground cinnamon
3 tablespoons butter, melted

Sauce

1/2 cup (1 stick) butter, softened
3/4 cup sugar
1/4 cup milk
6 tablespoons whiskey

◆ *For the pudding,* preheat the oven to 350 degrees. Soak the bread in the milk in a large bowl. Mix the sugar, eggs, walnuts, vanilla and cinnamon in a bowl. Pour the melted butter into a 9×13-inch baking pan and tilt the pan to coat. Spread the bread cubes and milk evenly in the pan. Pour the egg mixture over the top. Bake for 50 to 60 minutes. Cool slightly on a wire rack.

◆ *For the sauce,* beat the butter and sugar in a bowl. Stir in the milk and whiskey. Pour into a saucepan. Cook until heated through. Serve over the warm pudding.

A Southern man's preference at the end of a chilly day.

SERVES 12

Champions Dinner

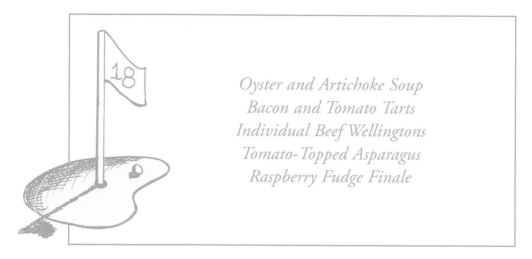

Oyster and Artichoke Soup
Bacon and Tomato Tarts
Individual Beef Wellingtons
Tomato-Topped Asparagus
Raspberry Fudge Finale

Golf's greatest players assemble on Tuesday evening of each Masters® Week for the Masters® Club dinner. Also called the Champions dinner, it is a tradition Ben Hogan started in 1952. The defending champion hosts and selects the menu for the esteemed gathering, where everyone in attendance is the owner of a Green Jacket.

That night, a dinner menu is chosen that reflects the tastes of the defending champion, although the Champions may choose from the regular Club menu as well. The menus have been as varied as the golfers themselves. Ben Crenshaw had barbecue brought in from Austin, Texas. Bernard Langer chose to serve German fare after his first Masters® win and presented a traditional Thanksgiving meal after his second victory. Nick Faldo chose fish and chips after his third win in 1996, and Mark O'Meara offered two of his favorites—sushi and fajitas! Vijay Singh selected a menu of traditional Thai delicacies for the 2001 dinner.

Our Champions dinner is composed of the leading recipes tested for this book—all received the highest ratings in testing. The recipes do ask for a little more effort from the cook, but are truly winners for your special-occasion table.

Each menu item should be considered a stand-alone specialty—bound to draw a legion of new fans! A stunning presentation places the Individual Beef Wellingtons in a class all their own, and the Raspberry Fudge Finale offers the pièce de résistance at the end of the evening.

As at the Masters® Club dinners where the conversation among men with a shared, treasured experience is prized, your Champions dinner can be a unique and memorable experience for your guests. You as the host must be available to partake in the experience, so be sure to prepare what you can in advance, as is recommended throughout our cookbook. The finest ingredients prepared with precision and care will speak to an event with polish and warmth, where your guests will declare *you* the champion of the kitchen.

Oyster and Artichoke Soup

3/4 cup (1¹/2 sticks) butter
1/2 cup each chopped celery and
  green bell pepper
1 cup chopped green onions
3 tablespoons all-purpose flour
1/4 cup cream sherry
1¹/2 teaspoons Worcestershire sauce
1¹/2 teaspoons seasoned salt

2 bay leaves
Pinch of thyme leaves
4 cups half-and-half, scalded
2 cups water
1 pint oysters, with their liquor
1¹/2 cups canned artichoke hearts,
  quartered, liquid reserved
Hot pepper sauce to taste

◆ Heat the butter in a large heavy saucepan over medium-high heat until beginning to brown.

◆ Finely dice the green peppers and celery in a food processor for 15 seconds. Add the green onions, celery and green pepper to the butter and saute for 1 minute. Stir in the flour. Cook for 8 to 10 minutes, stirring occasionally. Stir in the cream sherry, Worcestershire sauce, seasoned salt, bay leaves, thyme leaves, half-and-half and water. Bring to a low simmer and cook until thickened.

◆ Stir in the oysters and liquor and artichokes and reserved liquid and heat through. Season with hot pepper sauce. Remove the bay leaves.

—FRENCH MARKET GRILLE

A graciously shared signature recipe featured daily at the French Market Grille.

SERVES 12

Bacon and Tomato Tarts

3 tomatoes, chopped and drained
1 pound bacon, crisp-cooked and
  crumbled
1 cup mayonnaise
1¹/2 cups (6 ounces) shredded
  Swiss cheese

1 tablespoon Italian seasoning
1 Vidalia onion, chopped
2 (15-count) packages miniature
  phyllo shells

◆ Mix the tomatoes, bacon, mayonnaise, cheese, Italian seasoning and onion in a bowl.
Spoon into the phyllo shells. Arrange on a baking sheet. Bake at 350 degrees for 15 minutes
or until golden brown.

SERVES 30

THE QUINTESSENTIAL MASTERS® MEMORY IS 1986, WHEN JACK NICKLAUS
BECAME THE OLDEST CONTESTANT, AT AGE 46, TO WIN THE MASTERS®,
THANKS TO AN ABSOLUTELY MAGICAL SECOND NINE ON SUNDAY.
  "THE PLACE, THE NOSTALGIA, MY AGE," NICKLAUS RECALLS. "IT WAS
VERY SPECIAL, PROBABLY THE MOST SPECIAL WIN I'VE EVER HAD. AND
HAVING JACKIE ON THE BAG IS SOMETHING I'LL NEVER FORGET."

—JACK NICKLAUS, SIX-TIME MASTERS® CHAMPION
(1963, 1965, 1966, 1972, 1975, 1986)

Individual Beef Wellingtons with Mushroom Madeira Filling

6 (4- to 5-ounce) filets mignons

3/4 teaspoon fines herbes

Salt and freshly ground pepper
  to taste

4 1/2 teaspoons vegetable oil

1/2 cup chopped onion

1/2 cup chopped celery

1/2 cup chopped carrots

1 cup burgundy or other dry red wine

1 1/2 cups beef broth

2 tablespoons tomato paste

2 tablespoons cornstarch

1/4 cup madeira or other sweet wine

1 to 2 tablespoons butter

6 frozen patty shells, thawed

Mushroom Madeira Filling (page 165)

2 eggs, beaten

1 frozen patty shell, thawed (optional)

Fluted mushrooms for garnish

Chopped fresh parsley for garnish

◆ Arrange the filets in a shallow dish. Sprinkle with the fines herbes and season with salt and pepper. Heat the oil in a skillet. Add the onion, celery and carrots and sauté until tender. Remove from the heat and stir in the burgundy. Pour over the filets. Cover and marinate in the refrigerator for at least 2 hours.

◆ Prepare the Mushroom Madeira Filling (recipe below).

◆ Remove the filets to a plate and chill. Pour the marinade into a saucepan. Stir in the broth and tomato paste. Cover and simmer for 1 hour. Dissolve the cornstarch in the madeira in a small bowl. Stir into the broth mixture. Cook over medium heat until thickened, stirring constantly. Keep warm. Heat the butter in a nonstick skillet over medium-high heat. Sear the filets on both sides. Remove to a platter. Preheat the oven to 400 degrees.

◆ Roll each of 6 patty shells into a 7-inch square on a lightly floured work surface. Spread 1/3 cup of chilled Mushroom Filling in the center of each square. Top each with a filet. Brush the edges of the pastry with egg. Bring the sides of the dough together to enclose the filet and filling, pressing the edges to seal. Place seam side down on a rack in a broiler pan. Brush the top of each pastry with egg. Roll 1 patty shell to 1/8 inch on a lightly floured work surface. Cut into decorative shapes and arrange on top of each pastry. Brush with the remaining egg.
◆ Bake for 25 minutes or until golden brown. Serve with the madeira sauce and garnish with fluted mushrooms and chopped parsley.

SERVES 6

Mushroom Madeira Filling

2 tablespoons butter
1 pound fresh mushrooms,
   finely chopped
2 shallots, minced

3/4 teaspoon fines herbes
1/2 cup madeira or other sweet wine
Salt and pepper to taste

◆ Melt the butter in a large skillet over medium heat. Add the mushrooms, shallots and fines herbes and sauté until all liquid evaporates. Add the madeira and cook until all liquid evaporates, stirring occasionally. Season with salt and pepper. Remove to a bowl. Cover and chill thoroughly.

An exceptional entrée, well worth the effort. May be partially prepared ahead of time.

MAKES 2 CUPS

Tomato-Topped Asparagus

2 tablespoons olive oil

2 tablespoons cider vinegar

2 tablespoons chopped fresh basil

1/2 teaspoon salt

1/4 teaspoon sugar

1/8 teaspoon pepper

1 pound fresh asparagus

1/3 cup finely chopped tomato

Fresh basil sprigs for garnish

◆ Whisk the olive oil, vinegar, basil, salt, sugar and pepper in a bowl. Snap off the tough ends of the asparagus spears. Peel the scales with a knife or vegetable peeler, if desired. Place in a steamer basket over boiling water. Cover and steam for 4 to 6 minutes or until tender-crisp. Arrange the asparagus on a serving platter. Sprinkle the tomato down the center. Drizzle with the vinaigrette. Garnish with basil sprigs.

A premier vegetable highlighted by basil vinaigrette and fresh tomatoes.

SERVES 4

"THAT GREEN JACKET STANDS FOR A LOT MORE THAN JUST WINNING THE MASTERS®. THE MASTERS® JACKET EPITOMIZES PERFECTION IN GOLF."

—GARY PLAYER, THREE-TIME MASTERS® CHAMPION (1961, 1974, 1978)

Raspberry Fudge Finale

2 cups vanilla ice cream, softened
1/2 cup finely chopped toasted pecans
2 cups each raspberry sorbet and
    chocolate fudge ice cream, softened

Chocolate Sauce (below)
Fresh raspberries for garnish
Fresh mint sprigs for garnish

◆ Combine the vanilla ice cream and pecans in a bowl and stir to mix well. Spread in a 5×9-inch loaf pan lined with plastic wrap. Freeze for 30 minutes. Spread the raspberry sorbet over the vanilla ice cream. Freeze for 30 minutes. Spread the chocolate fudge ice cream over the raspberry layer. Cover and freeze 8 hours or until firm. Wrap a damp warm towel around loaf pan. Insert a sharp knife or small metal spatula around the edge to loosen the ice cream. Invert onto a cutting board. Remove the plastic wrap. Cut the loaf into 3/4-inch slices using an electric knife. Spoon the Chocolate Sauce onto dessert plates. Top each with a slice of ice cream. Garnish with fresh raspberries and mint sprigs. Serve immediately.

*Receive a standing ovation when you present this lavish dessert,
appealing to the eye and palate.*

SERVES 12

Chocolate Sauce

2 cups semisweet chocolate chips
1/4 cup (1/2 stick) butter
1/2 cup light corn syrup

1/2 cup water
1/4 cup raspberry schnapps or other
    raspberry-flavored liqueur

◆ Combine the chocolate chips and butter in the top of a double boiler. Cook over simmering water until melted, stirring frequently. Stir in the corn syrup, water and raspberry schnapps. Remove from the heat and let cool to room temperature.

MAKES 2 3/4 CUPS

The 19th Hole

Seared Scallops with Lemon and Dill
Cheesy Artichoke Bread
Hot Chicken and Sausage Dip
Cheesy Shrimp and Grits Casserole
Linguini with Chicken,
Garlic and Mushrooms
Lobster Ravioli in
Tomato Tarragon Cream
with Garlic Bread
Fettuccine Alfredo
Creamy Shrimp and Sausage Sauce
Pasta with Tomatoes and Artichokes
Rao's Chicken
Chicken Ribier
Hot Chicken Salad
Green Chicken Enchiladas
Chicken Puffs
Crab Cakes
Baked Fish Fillets
Macadamia-Crusted Grouper with
Peach and Mango Salsa

Flank Steak
Larry's Steak Marinade
Mexican Green Chile Strata
Asparagus Tart
Rice Pilaf
Gourmet Potatoes
Grilled Portobello Mushrooms with
Avocado and Goat Cheese
Tomato and Onion Salad
Spinach Cheese Soup
Sweet Potato Muffins
Broccoli Corn Bread
Fruit Surprise
Blueberry Pound Cake
Ice Cream Dessert
Heath Bars
Lemonade Icebox Pie
Chocolate Bread Pudding
Sally's Famous Chocolate Cake

The 19th Hole is a commonly used title, designation, or destination relating to the world of golf. It is often interpreted as a relaxing place to be at the end of a day spent on the golf course. After cooking your way through our 18-Hole-Course of Menus, we thought it only appropriate to offer you our own version of the 19th Hole. We hope you enjoy this collection of special recipes from golf pros and local restaurant pros, as well as Junior League entertaining pros.

Seared Scallops with Lemon and Dill

12 large sea scallops
Salt and pepper to taste
1 tablespoon butter
1/4 cup minced shallots
1 tablespoon butter
1/2 cup dry white wine

1 tablespoon chopped fresh dill
1 teaspoon grated lemon zest
1 tablespoon lemon juice
2 tablespoons chilled butter, cut into
  1/2-inch cubes

◆ Season the scallops with salt and pepper. Melt 1 tablespoon butter in a skillet over medium-high heat. Add the scallops and shallots and cook for 1 minute per side or just until the scallops are opaque in the center.

◆ Remove the scallops to a plate. Cover with foil and keep warm. Add 1 tablespoon butter to the skillet. Add the wine and cook for 1 minute or until reduced by half. Stir in the dill, lemon zest and lemon juice. Remove from the heat. Whisk in 2 tablespoons chilled butter a few cubes at a time. Season with salt and pepper. Pour over the scallops and serve.

A quick and easy appetizer. Serve with flair on a scallop shell.

SERVES 4

IN 1935, GENE SARAZEN HIT "THE SHOT HEARD ROUND THE WORLD," SCORING A DOUBLE EAGLE ON THE PAR FIVE 15TH HOLE, TYING CRAIG WOOD AND FORCING A PLAYOFF. SARAZEN WON THE 36-HOLE PLAYOFF THE FOLLOWING DAY BY FIVE STROKES.

Cheesy Artichoke Bread

1 (14-ounce) can artichoke hearts, drained and chopped
1 cup mayonnaise
1 garlic clove, minced

1 cup (4 ounces) grated Parmesan cheese
1 loaf French bread, halved lengthwise

◆ Preheat the oven to 350 degrees. Mix the artichoke hearts, mayonnaise, garlic and cheese in a bowl. Spread evenly on the bread and place on a baking sheet.
◆ Bake for 20 minutes or until golden brown and heated through. Cut crosswise into small slices and serve.

Very easy and always the first appetizer to disappear.

SERVES 8

Hot Chicken and Sausage Dip

16 ounces cream cheese, softened
3 scallions, finely chopped
1 pound sage sausage, cooked, drained and crumbled
1 (10-ounce) can chicken, drained

1 cup sour cream
1 tablespoon Worcestershire sauce
Dash of Tabasco sauce
Wheat Thins crackers

◆ Preheat the oven to 350 degrees. Combine the cream cheese, scallions, cooked sausage, chicken, sour cream, Worcestershire sauce and Tabasco sauce in a bowl. Stir to mix well. Spoon into a baking dish and cover.
◆ Bake for 30 minutes. Remove to a chafing dish and keep warm. Serve with the crackers.

SERVES 10

Cheesy Shrimp and Grits Casserole

4 cups chicken broth

1/2 teaspoon salt

1 cup grits

3/4 cup (3 ounces) each shredded sharp Cheddar cheese and Pepper Jack cheese

2 tablespoons butter

6 green onions, chopped

1 green bell pepper, chopped

1 garlic clove, minced

1 pound small shrimp, peeled and cooked

1 (10-ounce) can tomatoes with green chiles, drained

1/4 teaspoon each salt and pepper

1/4 cup (1 ounce) each shredded sharp Cheddar cheese and Pepper Jack cheese

◆ Bring the broth and 1/2 teaspoon salt to a boil in a large saucepan. Stir in grits, cover, reduce the heat, and simmer for 20 minutes. Stir in 3/4 cup Cheddar cheese and 3/4 cup Pepper Jack cheese. Remove to a large bowl.

◆ Preheat the oven to 350 degrees. Melt the butter in a large skillet over medium heat. Add the green onions, bell pepper and garlic and sauté for 5 minutes or until the vegetables are tender. Add to the grits mixture. Add the shrimp, tomatoes with green chiles, 1/4 teaspoon salt and pepper. Stir to mix well. Pour into a lightly greased 2-quart baking dish. Sprinkle with 1/4 cup Cheddar cheese and 1/4 cup Pepper Jack cheese. Bake for 35 to 45 minutes.

—CHARLES HOWELL III

SERVES 10 TO 12

"I'D PLAY IN THE MASTERS® IF THERE WERE NO SPONSORS, NO BROADCAST AND NO PURSE...THAT'S HOW MUCH I LOVE THE MASTERS®."

—CHARLES HOWELL III, AUGUSTA, GEORGIA, NATIVE, MADE HIS FIRST MASTERS® TOURNAMENT APPEARANCE IN 2002.

Linguini with Chicken, Garlic and Mushrooms

1/3 cup olive oil

1/4 cup minced garlic

3 pounds boneless chicken breasts, cut into bite-size pieces

2 to 3 poblano chiles, seeded and cut into thin 2-inch-long strips

8 ounces sliced fresh mushrooms

4 or 5 green onions, sliced

6 tablespoons white wine

6 Roma tomatoes, seeded and chopped

1/2 cup chopped fresh basil

2 to 3 tablespoons butter

1/2 cup grated fresh Parmesan cheese

Salt and pepper to taste

1 1/2 pounds fresh linguini, cooked

Additional grated fresh Parmesan cheese

◆ Heat the olive oil in a large skillet. Add the garlic and sauté until golden brown. Remove the garlic with a slotted spoon and set aside.

◆ Add the chicken to the hot oil. Sauté over medium heat for 5 minutes or until cooked through. Add the chiles, mushrooms and green onions and sauté for 2 to 3 minutes. Add the cooked garlic, wine, tomatoes and basil and sauté for 2 to 3 minutes.

◆ Remove from the heat and add the butter and 1/2 cup Parmesan cheese. Season with salt and pepper. Stir until the butter melts. Serve over the linguini on individual serving plates and sprinkle with Parmesan cheese.

A green salad and crusty bread may be added to complete the meal.

SERVES 8

Lobster Ravioli in Tomato Tarragon Cream Sauce

Fresh Pasta
3 cups semolina flour
1/2 cup all-purpose flour
1 teaspoon salt
4 eggs, slightly beaten
1/4 cup water
3 to 4 tablespoons olive oil

Lobster Filling
2 whole fresh lobsters,
   steamed for
   10 minutes
1 tablespoon chopped fresh
   chervil
1 tablespoon vanilla extract
Salt and pepper to taste

Tomato Tarragon Cream Sauce
4 cups heavy whipping cream
3 sprigs of fresh tarragon
1/4 teaspoon freshly ground
   nutmeg
1 large sweet onion, diced
1 tablespoon olive oil
2 (14-ounce) cans Italian-
   style tomatoes
4 ounces tomato paste
Salt and pepper to taste

◆ *For the pasta,* combine the semolina flour, all-purpose flour, salt, eggs, water and olive oil in a large bowl and mix well into a stiff dough. Knead for 10 minutes or until the dough is elastic. Wrap in plastic wrap and refrigerate for 20 minutes to rest. Cut the dough into pieces and roll into thin sheets as needed for making ravioli.

◆ *For the filling,* finely chop the lobster meat. Combine with the chervil and vanilla in a bowl. Season with salt and pepper.

◆ *For the Tomato Tarragon Cream Sauce,* bring the cream to a boil in a saucepan and reduce by 1/2, adding the tarragon and nutmeg as it boils. In another large saucepan, sauté the onion in the olive oil until translucent. Add the tomatoes and tomato paste. Simmer over medium heat until reduced by about 1/4. Season with salt and pepper. Let cool slightly and then purée. Strain the purée.

◆ Strain the reduced cream and combine with the tomato sauce. Set aside and keep warm.

◆ *To make the ravioli,* follow the directions on a ravioli press, or lay out 1 sheet. Place 1 teaspoon of filling every 2 inches; top with a second sheet. Press the sheets together around the mounds of filling; use a ravioli cutter or knife to cut out the squares.

◆ Bring a stockpot of water to a boil. Gently lower the ravioli into the water and cook for a couple of minutes, just until they float to the surface. Remove from the water with a slotted spoon. Serve with a generous helping of Tomato Tarragon Cream Sauce and Garlic Bread (below).

—DAVID LONG, PRIVATE CHEF TO THE PHIL AND AMY MICKELSON FAMILY

Phil's favorite, chosen as the featured entrée at the 2005 Champions dinner. Phil won his first major and first Green Jacket in 2004.

MAKES ABOUT 48 RAVIOLI, OR SERVES 4

Garlic Bread

1 pound (4 sticks) butter   1 loaf crusty bread
3 bulbs of garlic, cloves peeled

◆ Melt the butter with the garlic cloves in a large saucepan. Simmer until the garlic is very soft and the butter is nutty. Purée the mixture. Cut the loaf into slices, but don't cut all the way through. Spread the butter on both sides of each slice of bread. Toast in the oven until brown.

—DAVID LONG

MAKES I LOAF, ABOUT 20 SLICES

Fettuccine Alfredo

1/4 cup (1/2 stick) butter

2 garlic cloves, minced

1 pound fettuccini, cooked and
drained

1/2 cup (1 stick) butter

1/2 cup grated Parmesan cheese

1/2 cup chopped fresh parsley

1/2 cup half-and-half

Salt and freshly ground pepper
to taste

◆ Melt 1/4 cup butter in a large skillet. Add the garlic and sauté until tender. Add the fettuccini and toss to coat. Add 1/2 cup butter, the cheese, parsley and half-and-half. Season with salt and pepper. Toss until the butter melts and the sauce coats the pasta.

◆ Serve immediately on hot serving plates.

—MARIA FLOYD, WIFE OF RAYMOND FLOYD, 1976 MASTERS® CHAMPION

SERVES 4 TO 6

IN HIS WRITINGS, CLIFFORD ROBERTS USUALLY REFERRED TO THE GARMENT AS A "COAT" INSTEAD OF A "JACKET." BY WHATEVER NAME, THE MASTERS® COAT IS A THREE-BUTTON, SINGLE-BREASTED JACKET MADE FROM THREE YARDS OF TROPICAL-WEIGHT WOOL AND POLYESTER WITH A RAYON LINING.

Creamy Shrimp and Sausage Sauce

1 tablespoon vegetable oil
1 garlic clove, minced
2 shallots, chopped
8 ounces hot Italian sausage, casings removed
8 ounces sweet Italian sausage, casings removed
1 pound peeled shrimp

1 cup heavy whipping cream
2 (14-ounce) cans diced tomatoes
Basil to taste
Oregano to taste
Salt and pepper to taste
Hot cooked pasta or Parmesan cheese grits

✦ Heat the oil in a skillet. Add the garlic and shallots and sauté until tender. Add the hot sausage and sweet sausage and sauté until crumbly and cooked through. Add the shrimp and sauté just until the shrimp turn pink. Stir in the cream. Simmer for 2 minutes.

✦ Stir in the tomatoes. Season with basil, oregano, salt and pepper. Simmer for 10 to 15 minutes or until thickened.

✦ Serve over your favorite cooked pasta or Parmesan cheese grits.

Use all sweet sausage if serving small children. If serving all adults, add red pepper flakes, if desired.

SERVES 6

 PHIL MICKELSON IS THE SECOND CONSECUTIVE LEFT-HANDER TO WIN THE GREEN JACKET, SUCCEEDING CANADIAN MIKE WIER.

Pasta with Tomatoes and Artichokes

2 (6-ounce) jars marinated artichoke
  hearts
1/4 cup olive oil
1 large onion, chopped
2 or 3 garlic cloves, minced
1 teaspoon dried oregano
1 teaspoon dried basil

Salt to taste
Pinch of red pepper flakes
1 (28-ounce) can chopped Italian-style
  tomatoes
1/4 cup Parmesan cheese
8 ounces angel hair pasta, cooked
  and drained

◆ Drain the liquid from the artichoke hearts into a saucepan. Chop the artichoke hearts and set aside.

◆ Add the olive oil, onion, garlic, oregano, basil, salt and red pepper flakes to the saucepan. Cook over medium heat until onion and garlic are soft, about 10 minutes. Stir in the tomatoes. Cover and simmer for about 30 minutes.

◆ Add the cheese and artichoke hearts, stirring gently. Cook for 5 minutes. Pour the sauce over the cooked pasta and toss to combine.

Serve hot for a family dinner or cold for a luncheon.

SERVES 4

A TOTAL OF FIFTEEN DIFFERENT AWARDS AND TROPHIES CAN BE WON AT THE MASTERS®, RANGING FROM A REPLICA OF THE PERMANENT MASTERS® TROPHY, ON WHICH THE CHAMPION'S NAME IS ENGRAVED, TO A LARGE CRYSTAL BOWL FOR A HOLE-IN-ONE.

Rao's Chicken

2 cups bread crumbs
Dried parsley flakes, dried oregano,
    garlic powder, salt and pepper
    to taste

2 eggs
1/4 cup chicken broth
16 chicken thighs
Olive oil

◆ Season the bread crumbs with the next 5 ingredients in a shallow dish. Beat the eggs and broth in a shallow dish. Dip the chicken in the egg mixture and coat in the bread crumbs. Sprinkle olive oil on a baking sheet. Arrange the chicken, skin side up, on the baking sheet. Sprinkle with olive oil. Bake at 400 degrees for 11/2 hours or until cooked through.

—MARIA FLOYD

SERVES 8

Chicken Ribier

All-purpose flour for dredging
Salt and pepper to taste
4 boneless skinless chicken breasts
1/4 cup (1/2 stick) butter
1/2 cup dry white wine

20 seedless Ribier grapes
2 cups heavy whipping cream
Dash of Maggi seasoning sauce
    (optional)
Hot cooked fettuccini or rice pilaf

◆ Season the flour with salt and pepper in a shallow dish. Dredge the chicken in the flour. Melt the butter in a skillet. Add the chicken and sauté until almost cooked through. Add the wine and deglaze the skillet, stirring to scrape up the browned bits. Crush the grapes by hand over the skillet and add to the chicken. Stir in the cream and seasoning sauce. Cook until the sauce thickens. Serve over fettuccini or rice pilaf.

—SIXTH AT WATKINS

SERVES 4

Hot Chicken Salad

3 cups chopped cooked chicken
    breasts
1 cup slivered almonds
1 (8-ounce) can water chestnuts,
    drained and sliced
1 (2-ounce) jar diced pimentos,
    drained
2 cups chopped celery
1 teaspoon salt

$^{1}/_{2}$ teaspoon pepper
1 tablespoon lemon juice
1$^{1}/_{2}$ cups mayonnaise
1 cup (4 ounces) shredded sharp
    Cheddar cheese
1 (10-ounce) can condensed cream
    of chicken soup
1 (3-ounce) can French-fried onions

◆ Preheat the oven to 325 degrees. Combine the chicken, almonds, water chestnuts, pimentos, celery, salt, pepper, lemon juice, mayonnaise, cheese and chicken soup in a large bowl. Stir to mix well. Spoon into a 9×13-inch baking dish. Bake for 35 minutes. Sprinkle with the French-fried onions and bake for 10 minutes longer. Remove to a wire rack and let stand for 10 minutes before serving.

—BARBARA NICKLAUS

"Men love it!"

SERVES 8

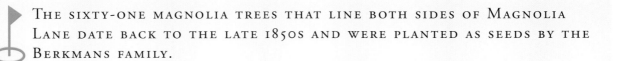

THE SIXTY-ONE MAGNOLIA TREES THAT LINE BOTH SIDES OF MAGNOLIA LANE DATE BACK TO THE LATE 1850S AND WERE PLANTED AS SEEDS BY THE BERKMANS FAMILY.

Green Chicken Enchiladas

3 tablespoons butter
1 yellow onion, chopped
16 ounces cream cheese
Salt and pepper to taste
2 (4-ounce) cans chopped
    green chiles
1 tablespoon cumin
2 pounds boneless skinless chicken
    breasts, cooked and shredded
3 tablespoons butter
6 tablespoons all-purpose flour

2 cups heavy whipping cream
2 (4-ounce) cans chopped green chiles
1 tablespoon cumin
2 (10-ounce) cans tomatoes with
    green chiles, drained
24 (8-inch) flour or corn tortillas
2 cups (8 ounces) Monterey Jack
    cheese, shredded
1 cup (4 ounces) grated fresh
    Parmesan cheese

◆ *For the filling,* melt 3 tablespoons butter in a large saucepan. Add the onion and sauté until tender but not browned. Add the cream cheese and cook until softened, stirring often. Season with salt and pepper. Stir in 2 cans green chiles, 1 tablespoon cumin and the chicken. Remove from the heat and set aside.

◆ *For the sauce,* melt 3 tablespoons butter in a saucepan. Stir in the flour. Cook for a few minutes, stirring constantly. Stir in the cream gradually. Cook until thickened, stirring constantly. Stir in 2 cans green chiles and 1 tablespoon cumin. Season with salt and pepper.

◆ Spread the tomatoes with green chiles in 2 flat-bottomed 2-quart baking dishes. Soften 1 tortilla briefly in a hot skillet. Remove to a work surface and top with some of the filling. Roll up and place, seam side down, in the baking dish. Repeat with the remaining tortillas and filling.

◆ Pour the sauce over the enchiladas and sprinkle with the Monterey Jack cheese and Parmesan cheese. Bake at 350 degrees until the cheese melts and the top is golden brown.

—POPPYSEEDS

SERVES 12

Chicken Puffs

Puffs

3 ounces cream cheese, softened
2 tablespoons margarine, melted
2 cups chopped cooked chicken
2 tablespoons milk
1/4 teaspoon salt
1/8 teaspoon pepper
1 (8-ounce) can refrigerator
   crescent rolls
Poppy seeds

Gravy

2 tablespoons margarine
2 tablespoons all-purpose flour
1 cup chicken broth
Salt and pepper to taste

◆ *For the puffs,* mix the cream cheese and melted margarine in a bowl. Add the chicken, milk, salt and pepper. Stir to mix well. Cover and chill overnight, if desired. Preheat the oven to 350 degrees. Unroll the crescent roll dough on a work surface. Separate into 4 squares, pressing the seams to seal. Spoon 1/2 cup of the chicken mixture in the center of each square. Pull the opposite corners of dough together over the filling and twist to seal. Arrange on an ungreased baking sheet. Sprinkle with poppy seeds. Bake for 20 minutes or until golden brown.

◆ *For the gravy,* combine the margarine and flour in a skillet. Cook over medium-high heat until bubbly and browned, stirring constantly with a fork. Stir in the broth slowly. Reduce the heat and simmer until thickened. Season with salt and pepper. Serve with the chicken puffs.

Comfort food at its finest, and the puffs are adorable.

SERVES 4

Crab Cakes

1 tablespoon mayonnaise
1 egg
1 (16-ounce) can lump crab meat, drained and flaked
1/2 red bell pepper, finely chopped

1/2 green bell pepper, finely chopped
Salt and pepper to taste
1/2 cup bread crumbs
Butter

◆ Beat the mayonnaise and egg in a bowl. Add the crab meat, red bell pepper and green bell pepper. Season with salt and pepper. Stir gently to mix. Shape into 4 crab cakes. Coat with the bread crumbs. Arrange on a baking sheet. Broil for 8 minutes. Dot each crab cake with butter and broil for 3 minutes longer.

—MARIA FLOYD

SERVES 4

Baked Fish Fillets

1 1/2 pounds orange roughy or tilapia fillets
1 cup sour cream
1/4 cup shredded Parmesan cheese
1/2 teaspoon paprika

1/2 teaspoon salt
1/4 teaspoon pepper
2 tablespoons Italian-style seasoned bread crumbs
2 tablespoons melted butter

◆ Preheat the oven to 350 degrees. Arrange the fillets in a single layer in a greased 9×13-inch baking pan. Combine the sour cream, cheese, paprika, salt and pepper in a small bowl. Stir to mix well. Spread the mixture evenly over the fish. Sprinkle with bread crumbs and drizzle with the melted butter. Bake for 20 to 25 minutes or until the fish flakes easily.

—BONNIE MIZE

SERVES 4

Macadamia-Crusted Grouper with Peach and Mango Salsa

2 eggs
1/2 cup milk
2 cups all-purpose flour
Salt and pepper to taste
1 cup macadamia nuts, crushed

4 grouper fillets
Olive oil
1 to 2 tablespoons butter
Peach and Mango Salsa (page 185)
Chopped fresh cilantro

◆ Preheat the oven to 350 degrees.

◆ Beat the eggs and milk in a shallow dish. Season the flour with salt and pepper in a shallow dish. Spread the macadamia nuts in a shallow dish. Dredge the grouper in the flour mixture, shaking off any excess. Dip in the egg mixture and then in the macadamia nuts to coat on all sides.

◆ Heat olive oil and 1 tablespoon butter in a skillet over medium-high heat. Add 2 fillets to the skillet. Cook for 3 to 4 minutes per side, turning once, or until the macadamia nut coating is lightly browned. Remove to a baking dish. Add olive oil and 1 tablespoon butter to the skillet, if needed. Add the remaining fillets and cook as above.

◆ Brush the fillets with olive oil. Bake for 8 to 10 minutes or until the fish flakes easily. Remove to serving plates and top with Peach and Mango Salsa. Sprinkle with chopped cilantro.

—GREG AND LAURA NORMAN

SERVES 4

Peach and Mango Salsa

2 peaches
1 mango
1 bunch fresh cilantro, chopped
1 tablespoon diced red onion

Juice of $1/2$ lemon
3 tablespoons olive oil
Salt and pepper to taste

◆ Peel, pit and chop the peaches into small cubes, saving any juice. Peel, pit and chop the mango into small cubes, saving any juice. Combine the peaches and juice, mango and juice, cilantro, onion, lemon juice and olive oil in a bowl. Season with salt and pepper. Toss to mix. Cover and chill for 20 minutes to blend the flavors.

SERVES 4

"THROUGH THE YEARS, THE MASTERS® HAS VERY MUCH CHANGED MY LIFE. IT HAS GIVEN ME MANY WONDERFUL MEMORIES, AS WELL AS A FEW DIFFICULT ONES, BUT I HAVE EXTRACTED A STRONG SENSE OF PRIDE FROM AUGUSTA NATIONAL. TO THIS DAY, I CONTINUE TO RECEIVE LETTERS FROM MY FANS REGARDING THE MANNER IN WHICH I HANDLED DEFEAT AT THE TOURNAMENT I DESPERATELY WANTED TO WIN. SO, IN MY MIND, I HAVE ACHIEVED VICTORY AT THE MASTERS® THROUGH DEFEAT."

—GREG NORMAN, CO-HOLDER OF THE MASTERS® TOURNAMENT RECORD FOR 18 HOLES, AT 63

Flank Steak

1¹/2 to 2 pounds flank steak
2 tablespoons dry sherry
2 tablespoons soy sauce
1 tablespoon honey
1 tablespoon sugar

2 teaspoons unseasoned meat
  tenderizer
1 teaspoon salt
1 teaspoon MSG

◆ Pierce the steak with a fork several times and place in a baking dish. Whisk the sherry, soy sauce, honey, sugar, meat tenderizer, salt and MSG in a small bowl. Pour the marinade over the steak and turn to coat. Cover and marinate in the refrigerator for at least 3 hours.
◆ Remove the steak and discard the marinade. Broil or grill the steak for 7 minutes per side or to desired doneness.

SERVES 6 TO 8

Larry's Steak Marinade

¹/3 cup red wine vinegar
3 tablespoons ketchup
2 tablespoons vegetable oil
1 tablespoon soy sauce
1 tablespoon Worcestershire sauce

1 teaspoon dry mustard
1 teaspoon salt
¹/4 teaspoon pepper
2 garlic cloves, pressed
4 to 6 steaks

◆ Whisk the vinegar, ketchup, oil, soy sauce, Worcestershire sauce, dry mustard, salt, pepper and garlic in a small bowl. Place the steaks in a sealable plastic bag. Add the marinade and seal the bag. Marinate in the refrigerator for at least 30 minutes. Remove the steaks and let come to room temperature. Discard the marinade. Grill the steaks to desired doneness.

—LARRY MIZE

SERVES 4 TO 6

Mexican Green Chile Strata

6 slices firm white bread, crusts
  removed
Softened butter
2 cups (8 ounces) shredded sharp
  Cheddar cheese
2 cups (8 ounces) shredded Monterey
  Jack cheese
2 (4-ounce) cans chopped
  green chiles

6 eggs
2 cups milk
2 teaspoons salt
2 teaspoons paprika
1 teaspoon oregano
1/2 teaspoon garlic powder
1/4 teaspoon dry mustard
1/4 teaspoon pepper

◆ Spread 1 side of each bread slice with butter. Arrange the bread, buttered side down, in a 9×12-inch baking pan. Sprinkle with the Cheddar cheese and Monterey Jack cheese. Sprinkle the green chiles evenly over the cheese. Beat the eggs, milk, salt, paprika, oregano, garlic powder, dry mustard and pepper in a bowl. Pour evenly over the cheese mixture. Cover and chill overnight.

◆ Remove from the refrigerator 30 minutes prior to baking. Preheat the oven to 325 degrees. Bake, uncovered, for 50 minutes or until lightly browned. Remove to a wire rack and let cool for 10 minutes before serving.

Fresh fruit will complement the flavors of this breakfast entrée.

SERVES 8

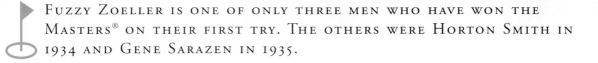

FUZZY ZOELLER IS ONE OF ONLY THREE MEN WHO HAVE WON THE MASTERS® ON THEIR FIRST TRY. THE OTHERS WERE HORTON SMITH IN 1934 AND GENE SARAZEN IN 1935.

Asparagus Tart

1 (1-crust) refrigerator pie pastry
1 teaspoon all-purpose flour
14 ounces fresh asparagus, trimmed
   and cut into 3-inch spears
2 eggs
2/3 cup half-and-half

1/2 cup grated Parmesan cheese
1 tablespoon chopped fresh tarragon
   or 1 teaspoon dried tarragon
1/2 teaspoon salt
Pepper to taste

◆ Preheat the oven to 450 degrees.
◆ Unfold the pie pastry on a work surface and press to seal any cracks. Sprinkle with the flour and rub the flour into the dough. Fit the pastry, floured side down, into a 9-inch tart pan with a removable bottom. Fold the edges under and crimp. Pierce the dough several times with a fork. Bake for 15 minutes or until golden brown. Remove to a wire rack to cool.
◆ Reduce the oven temperature to 350 degrees. Cook the asparagus in a saucepan of boiling salted water for 4 minutes or until tender-crisp. Drain well and place on paper towels.
◆ Beat the eggs, half-and-half, cheese, tarragon and salt in a bowl. Season with pepper. Arrange the asparagus spoke-fashion in the baked crust, with the tops towards the outside and the ends meeting in the center. Pour the egg mixture evenly over the asparagus. Bake for 35 minutes or until puffed and golden brown. Remove to a wire rack and let cool slightly. Loosen from the side of the pan with a sharp knife and remove the tart.

A tart pan is not a necessity; a pie plate can be used.

SERVES 4 TO 6

AUGUSTA NATIONAL PLAYED HOST TO THE FIRST PGA SENIORS CHAMPIONSHIP IN 1937.

Rice Pilaf

1/2 cup (1 stick) butter
1/2 onion, chopped
3/4 teaspoon each paprika and oregano
8 ounces fresh mushrooms, sliced

3/4 cup each rice and water
1/2 cup sherry
1 (10-ounce) can condensed beef
  consommé

◆ Melt the butter in a saucepan. Stir in the onion, paprika, oregano, mushrooms and rice. Simmer for 20 minutes. Remove to a baking dish. Stir in the water, sherry and consommé. Bake, covered, at 400 degrees for 45 minutes. Uncover and bake for 15 minutes longer.

—BARBARA NICKLAUS

"I never serve this without someone asking for the recipe."

SERVES 6

Gourmet Potatoes

8 unpeeled potatoes
1/4 cup (1/2 stick) butter
2 cups (8 ounces) shredded Cheddar
  cheese

1 1/2 cups sour cream
1/3 cup chopped green onions
1 teaspoon salt
1/2 teaspoon pepper

◆ Preheat the oven to 325 degrees. Bring the potatoes and enough water to cover to a boil in a saucepan. Cook until tender. Drain and let cool. Peel and coarsely shred the potatoes. Melt the butter and cheese in a large saucepan, stirring constantly. Stir in the remaining ingredients. Fold in the shredded potatoes. Spoon into a greased 2-quart baking dish. Bake for 25 minutes.

Shredding the potatoes is the key to making this recipe a special side dish.

SERVES 8

Grilled Portobello Mushrooms with Avocado and Goat Cheese

4 large portobello mushroom caps
2 tablespoons white wine
1 tablespoon olive oil
1 tablespoon minced garlic
3/4 teaspoon kosher salt
1/2 teaspoon freshly ground pepper

1/2 teaspoon chopped fresh oregano
1 avocado, thinly sliced
1 yellow tomato, thinly sliced
1 roasted red pepper, julienned
4 ounces fresh goat cheese
1 head frisée lettuce

◆ Arrange the mushroom caps in a shallow dish. Whisk the wine, olive oil, garlic, salt, pepper and oregano in a small bowl. Pour over the mushroom caps and let marinate for 30 minutes. Remove the mushrooms and discard the marinade. Grill the mushrooms over a medium-hot fire (preferably a wood fire) for about 3 minutes or until tender, turning several times. Remove to a broiler pan. Stack avocado, then tomato and then roasted pepper in each mushroom cap. Cut the cheese into thin slices with a hot knife and place on top. Broil until the cheese melts and is light brown. Serve on lettuce-lined plates. Top each with a stacked mushroom cap.

—MARIA FLOYD

SERVES 4

Tomato and Onion Salad

Beefsteak tomatoes, sliced
Vidalia or Bermuda onions, sliced
Crumbled bleu cheese

Vinaigrette salad dressing
Salt and pepper to taste

◆ Layer tomatoes and onions on a salad plate. Sprinkle with bleu cheese. Pour the desired amount of salad dressing over the top. Season with salt and pepper.

—ARNOLD PALMER

Spinach Cheese Soup

2 tablespoons vegetable oil
3/4 cup chopped onion
1 garlic clove, minced
6 cups water
6 chicken bouillon cubes
8 ounces fine noodles
6 cups milk
2 (10-ounce) packages frozen chopped
   spinach, thawed

3 cups (12 ounces) Cheddar cheese,
   shredded
3 cups (12 ounces) Swiss cheese,
   shredded
1 teaspoon salt
Croutons

◆ Heat the oil in a large stockpot. Add the onion and garlic and sauté until tender. Add the water and bouillon cubes. Bring to a boil. Stir in the noodles slowly so that the soup continues to boil. Cook for 6 minutes. Reduce the heat and stir in the milk, spinach, Cheddar cheese, Swiss cheese and salt. Cook until heated through, stirring frequently; do not boil. Sprinkle with croutons before serving.

Great for a crowd, a favorite of our sustaining members!

SERVES 10

"YOU SEE, NO OTHER TOURNAMENT IN THE WORLD HAS AS MUCH RESPECT FOR TRADITION AND THE PEOPLE WHO SHAPED IT. YOU CAN SEE EVIDENCE OF IT EVERYWHERE, FROM THE CHAMPIONS DINNER TO THE HONORARY STARTERS CEREMONY TO THE LANDMARKS SPRINKLED ABOUT THE COURSE. THE TOURNAMENT'S EMPHASIS ON HISTORY AND TRADITION HAS ENRICHED THE EXPERIENCE FOR BOTH FANS AND PLAYERS, MAKING IT UNIQUE IN SPORTS."

—ARNOLD PALMER, 4 TIME MASTERS® CHAMPION (1958, 1960, 1962, 1964)

Sweet Potato Muffins

1¹/2 cups all-purpose flour
2 teaspoons baking powder
1 teaspoon ground cinnamon
¹/2 teaspoon nutmeg
¹/4 teaspoon salt
¹/2 cup (1 stick) butter, softened
1¹/4 cups sugar

2 eggs
1¹/4 cups mashed cooked sweet
  potatoes
1 cup milk
¹/4 cup chopped pecans
2 tablespoons sugar
¹/4 teaspoon ground cinnamon

◆ Preheat the oven to 400 degrees.

◆ Sift the flour, baking powder, 1 teaspoon cinnamon, the nutmeg and salt together.

◆ Beat the butter and 1¹/4 cups sugar in a bowl until light and fluffy. Beat in the eggs. Stir in the sweet potatoes. Stir in the dry ingredients alternately with the milk just until mixed; do not overmix. Fold in the pecans. Fill greased muffin cups 2/3 full.

◆ Mix 2 tablespoons sugar and ¹/4 teaspoon cinnamon in a small bowl. Sprinkle over the muffins. Bake for 20 to 25 minutes or until the muffins test done. Remove to a wire rack to cool.

Perfect for a luncheon, a wonderful accompaniment with soup.

MAKES I DOZEN MUFFINS

"AFTER FIFTY YEARS, I HAVE SO MANY FOND MEMORIES OF THE MASTERS® TOURNAMENT AND THE CITY OF AUGUSTA THAT I COULD FILL A BOOK WRITING ABOUT THEM, BUT I'LL NEVER FORGET THE THRILL OF DRIVING DOWN MAGNOLIA LANE FOR THE FIRST TIME IN 1955."

—ARNOLD PALMER, AFTER PLAYING IN HIS 50TH CONSECUTIVE MASTERS® IN 2004

Broccoli Corn Bread

3 eggs, beaten
2 (8-ounce) packages
   corn bread mix
2 cups (8 ounces) Cheddar cheese,
   shredded

1 (10-ounce) package frozen chopped
   broccoli, thawed and drained
3/4 cup cottage cheese
1 tablespoon grated Parmesan cheese

◆ Preheat the oven to 350 degrees. Combine all the ingredients in a bowl and mix well. Pour into a nonstick 9×13-inch baking pan. Bake for 20 minutes or until a wooden pick inserted in the center comes out clean. Remove to a wire rack to cool. Cut into squares and serve.

SERVES 10 TO 12

Fruit Surprise

1 cup seedless red grapes, halved
1 cup fresh blueberries
1 cup fresh strawberries, halved

1 cup chopped fresh peaches
1 cup packed brown sugar
2 cups sour cream

◆ Mix the grapes, blueberries, strawberries and peaches in a 9×13-inch baking dish and spread evenly in the bottom. Sprinkle with the brown sugar. Spread the sour cream evenly over the brown sugar. Cover and chill for at least 3 hours or up to 8 hours.
◆ Spoon into glass serving dishes. *(Use only fresh fruit in this recipe, not frozen or canned.)*

—BONNIE MIZE

"We love to make this in the summer, especially around the Fourth of July!"

SERVES 8

Blueberry Pound Cake

1 cup (2 sticks) butter, softened
2 cups sugar
4 eggs, at room temperature
1 teaspoon vanilla extract
3 cups all-purpose flour

1 teaspoon baking powder
1 teaspoon salt
1 cup fresh blueberries
Additional sugar

◆ Preheat the oven to 325 degrees. Beat 1 cup butter and 2 cups sugar in a large bowl with an electric mixer until light and fluffy. Beat in the eggs 1 at a time. Beat in the vanilla. Add the flour 1 cup at a time, beating well after each addition. Add the baking powder and salt and beat for 2 minutes. The batter will be very thick. Fold in the blueberries.
◆ Butter two 5×9-inch loaf pans. Sprinkle with sugar. Spread the batter in the pans. Sprinkle additional sugar over the top. Bake for 1 hour or until the loaves test done. Remove to a wire rack to cool.

The sugar topping adds a sweet surprise!

MAKES 2 LOAVES

Ice Cream Dessert

Häagen-Dazs vanilla ice cream
Godiva Chocolate Liqueur

Whipped cream
Maraschino cherry

◆ Spoon ice cream into an individual dessert bowl. Pour the desired amount of chocolate liqueur over the ice cream. Top with whipped cream and a cherry.

—ARNOLD PALMER

A classic dessert from a classic gentleman!

SERVES I

Heath Bars

Club crackers
1 cup (2 sticks) butter

1 cup packed brown sugar
2 cups chocolate chips

◆ Preheat the oven to 350 degrees. Fit a single layer of crackers in a foil-lined 13×18-inch baking pan.
◆ Melt the butter in a saucepan over low heat. Add the brown sugar and cook until dissolved, stirring constantly. Pour evenly over the cracker layer. Bake for 5 to 7 minutes.
◆ Sprinkle the chocolate chips over the top and let stand until melted. Spread the chocolate evenly to the edges of the pan. Chill until hardened. Break into pieces. Can be frozen.

—SALLY IRWIN, WIFE OF HALE IRWIN, PARTICIPANT IN
OVER 20 MASTERS® TOURNAMENTS

SERVES 12

Lemonade Icebox Pie

1 (6-ounce) can frozen lemonade
concentrate, slightly thawed
2 cups vanilla ice cream, softened

8 ounces whipped topping
1 (9-inch) graham cracker pie shell

◆ Beat the lemonade in a bowl with an electric mixer at low speed for 30 seconds. Beat in the ice cream gradually. Fold in the whipped topping. Spoon into the pie shell. Freeze until firm, at least 4 hours. Let stand at room temperature for 15 to 20 minutes before cutting.

For individual treats, spoon the mixture into miniature phyllo shells and freeze. This can also be made with raspberry lemonade and garnished with fresh raspberries.

SERVES 8

Chocolate Bread Pudding

6 large croissants, cut into
   1-inch pieces
3 cups milk
3 cups heavy whipping cream
1 cup sugar
1 tablespoon vanilla extract

12 eggs
1 cup sugar
1 cup semisweet chocolate chips
1 (15-ounce) jar caramel ice cream
   topping

◆ Preheat oven to 350 degrees. Spread the croissant pieces on a baking sheet. Bake for 5 minutes or until lightly toasted. Let cool. Combine the milk, cream and 1 cup sugar in a saucepan. Bring to a simmer over medium heat, stirring until the sugar dissolves. Simmer for 5 minutes. Remove from the heat and stir in the vanilla. Whisk the eggs and 1 cup sugar in a large bowl. Whisk in the hot milk mixture gradually. Spread the croissant pieces in a 9×13-inch baking pan. Sprinkle with the chocolate chips. Pour the egg mixture evenly over the top. Let stand for 30 to 60 minutes. Place the baking pan in a larger pan. Add enough very hot water to the larger pan to come 1 inch up the sides of the baking pan. Bake for 45 minutes. Remove to a wire rack to cool. Serve with the caramel topping.

*Made with croissants and sprinkled with chocolate chips,
this bread pudding is sure to please.*

SERVES 12

Sally's Famous Chocolate Cake

Cake

2 cups sugar
2 cups all-purpose flour
1 teaspoon each baking soda and salt
1 cup (2 sticks) margarine
1 cup water
1/4 cup baking cocoa
1/2 cup sour cream
2 eggs
1 teaspoon vanilla extract

Icing

1/2 cup (1 stick) margarine
1/4 cup baking cocoa
6 tablespoons sour cream
1 (16-ounce) package confectioners' sugar
1 teaspoon vanilla extract
Vanilla ice cream
Chocolate sauce

◆ *For the cake,* preheat the oven to 350 degrees. Sift the sugar, flour, baking soda and salt into a large bowl. Bring the margarine and water to a boil in a saucepan. Remove from the heat and stir in the baking cocoa. Stir into the dry ingredients. Beat in the sour cream, eggs and vanilla until smooth. Pour into a greased 13×18-inch baking pan. Bake for 15 to 20 minutes or until a wooden pick inserted in the center comes out clean; do not overbake.

◆ *For the icing,* combine the margarine, baking cocoa and sour cream in a saucepan. Bring to a boil. Remove from the heat and add the confectioners' sugar and vanilla. Beat until smooth. Pour immediately over the warm cake. Serve with vanilla ice cream and chocolate sauce.

—SALLY IRWIN

SERVES 12

 "OVER THE YEARS, WE HAVE SO ENJOYED COMING TO AUGUSTA FOR THE MASTERS®. THE GOLF COURSE IS OUTSTANDING, THE CITY IS BEAUTIFUL, AND THE PEOPLE ARE GRACIOUS IN THEIR HOSPITALITY."

—SALLY AND HALE IRWIN

Cookbook Development Committee

Catharine Lemmon
CHAIRMAN, 2004-2005

Ellen Pruitt
CHAIRMAN, 2003-2004
SUSTAINING ADVISOR 2004-2005

Tammy Fuqua
VICE CHAIRMAN

Lisa Whatley, ART AND DESIGN CHAIRMAN
Amanda Williams
Jennifer Ellis
Susan Prather
Jenny Storer

Jill Dromsky, NON-RECIPE TEXT CHAIRMAN
Melissa Hankinson
Ann Beth Rutkowski, CONTRIBUTING WRITER

Rachel Partl, RECIPE MANAGER 2004-2005
Sandy Olandt, RECIPE MANAGER 2003-2004
Pam Rinker, TESTING COORDINATOR

MARKETING COMMITTEE
Katie Holt
Hallie Merry
Alison Andrews

Jennifer Hamilton, LAUNCH PARTY CHAIRMAN
Elizabeth Donsbach
Margaret Helton
Katy Ledford

Special Acknowledgments

Our deepest appreciation goes to photographer Todd Bennett, whose knowledge, insight, and kindness have helped us create a wonderful array of photographs.

A debt of gratitude to the following, who generously opened their homes and property to the Junior League of Augusta, Georgia, for photography locations:

Adair & B.J. Blackwood

Clarence & Julie Blalock

Chuck & Tammy Fuqua

Will & Janet McKnight

Lionel & Susan Prather

Ernie & Allison Sizemore

Georgia Golf Hall of Fame &

Botanical Gardens

The Old Government House

The Junior League of Augusta, Georgia, is grateful to the following businesses, who donated items for our photographs:

Aarbour Pool and Patio

American Wilderness Outfitters Ltd.

Angevine's Fine Silver and Gifts

Design Images & Gifts

Doris Diamonds

Events 20–20 Catering

Fat Man's Forest

Lady Banks Flowers and Company

The Swank Co.

Villa

Thank you to Dorinda P. Carver, the artist who created custom artwork for our chapter dividers.

A special thank-you to the Sustainer Advisory Council, which provided wisdom, experience, and support to our committee for two years:

Mary Ann Baggs

Jackie Blanchard

Karin Calloway

Marian Clark

Freddie Flynt

Shelley Harris

Toni Peacock

Betty Powell

Ellen Pruitt

Sabrina Rush

Anne Trotter

Louise Vallotton

Contributors

Thank you to the following, who have provided support and contributed to our cookbook in so many ways, including submitting recipes, testing, and tasting.

Harry Adams	Amy Caplan	Becky Echols	Laurie Haynie
Margaret Somers Anderson	Courtnay Capps	Katy Eisert	Lori Holley
Miriam Atkins	Niti Carlson	Susan Evans	Charles Howell III
Mary Ann Baggs	Caroline Caveney	Indee Few	Debbie Howell
Angela Bakke	Mary Linda Chambers	Sherry Fleming	Jane Howington
Pam Balk	Melinda Chapman	Ray & Maria Floyd	Jodi Huff
Lora Barnbrook	Marian Clark	Freddie Flynt	Beth Huggins
Charlotte Barrett	Townsend Clarkson	Carla Ford	Hale & Sally Irwin
Marquin Barrett	Ivey Coleman	Karen Foushee	Sterling Ivey
Deborah Bates	Lisa Curley	Jean Franke	Megan Jackson
Kim Beavers	Susan Darby	French Market Grille	Cammie Jones
Kathy Beeson	Floride Dickert	Tammy Fuqua	Donna Jones
Patti Bennett	Kelly Dippolito	Rechelle Garmany	Karen Jones
Cindy Bitting	Elizabeth Donsbach	Corinee Garris	Maureen Jones
Jackie Blanchard	Martha Donsbach	Nancy Gentas	Susan Jordan
Cathy Boone	Theckla Donsbach	Nancy Gentry	Elizabeth Kane
Carrie Brigham	Marcia Doris	Maria Greenway	Julia Key
Dianne Brown	Maude Doris	Lynn Hackett	Marjorie Kilchenstein
Kay Bryant	Mary Anne Douglass	Betty Hanks	April King
Ivenchie Bush	Jill Dromsky	Marsha Hannay	Edythe King
Cadwalladers Café	Jean Duncan	Gracie Harison	Andria Kuzeff
Karin Calloway	Dana Duvall	Julie Harison	Shannon Lanier
Calvert's	Lucinda Eaves	Harry & Merry Harper	Katy Ledford
Martha Caper	Jackie Echelberger	Shelley Harris	Catharine Lemmon

Karen Leopard
Chef David Long
Lillian Magruder
Amanda Martin
Lee Anne Martin
Ruth Masella
Thayer McGahee
Connie McMillan
Juli Means
Laura Melbourne
Robin Merriman
Charlotte Merry
Hallie Merry
Phil & Amy Mickelson
Mary Ashton Mills
Edie Miller
Larry & Bonnie Mize
Mickey Montevideo
Laura Morris
Laura Mulloy
Lisa Myrick
April Neel
Marla Nelson
Jack & Barbara Nicklaus

Tricia Nixon
Greg & Laura Norman
Katherine Normon
Amy Oetting
Sandy Olandt
Ann O'Neal
Molly Osteen
Arnold Palmer
Kay Parker
Rachel Partl
Nancy Payne
Toni Peacock
Geoff Perry
Cathy Pitock
Poppyseeds
Mary Porter
Betty Powell
Jackie Prather
Susan Prather
Pauline S. Raffety
Jeanie Reeder
John D. & Harriet Reynolds
Pam Rinker
Holly Rippy

Kathryn Rogers
Tina Rojas
Emily Ross
Rebecca Rule
Ann Beth Rutkowski
Tara Sanders
Daryn Sasser
Natalie Schweers
Patricia Moore Shaffer
Donald Shapiro
Pat Shelton
Anne Sherman
Ginger Simms
Sixth at Watkins
Ann Smith
Betty Snelling
Maryan St. Onge
Jenny Stanley
Jane Starnes
Helen Stephens
Amanda Sterner
Tracy Stolarski
Jenny Elliott Storer
Nancy Story

Paul & Jan Stuntz
Sundial Garden Club
Anne Thurmond
Stacy Townsend
Anne Trotter
Kim Trotter
Louise Vallotton
Lucy Weigle
Lisa Whatley
Amanda Williams
Barbara Williams
Margaret Williams
Elizabeth Wood
Kelli Wright
Barb Wright
Dianne Wright
Avis Yount

Index

Almonds
Almond Raisin Rice, 121
Almond Toffee, 132
Glazed Almond Cake, 65

Appetizers. *See also* Dips;
   Salsa; Spreads
Artichoke Spinach Pinwheels, 122
Bacon and Tomato Tarts, 163
Bacon-Wrapped Water
   Chestnuts, 78
Bleu Cheese Iced Grapes, 79
Boiled Peanuts, 154
Corinee's Cheese Straws, 24
Crab and Corn-Filled Endive, 94
Crostini with Mushrooms, 68
Fried Green Tomatoes, 102
Herbed Cheesecake, 77
Italian Cheese Torta, 69
Kahlúa Pecan Brie, 16
Marinated Broccoli and
   Cauliflower, 80
Mustard-Marinated Shrimp, 14
Not Your Momma's
   Deviled Eggs, 26
Olive Cups, 115
Salmon Roll-Ups, 79
Scallop Shooters in
   Saffron Cream, 116
Seared Scallops with Lemon
   and Dill, 170
Shrimp and Artichoke Hearts, 78
Spinach Squares, 44
Tomato Poppers, 32
Warm Goat Cheese Toasts, 33

Apples
Apple Dip, 153
Curried Kidney Beans, 157

Red Delicious Cheese Spread, 40
Tangy Apple Salad, 110

Artichokes
Artichoke Salsa, 51
Artichoke Spinach Pinwheels, 122
Cheesy Artichoke Bread, 171
Oyster and Artichoke Soup, 162
Pasta with Tomatoes and
   Artichokes, 178
Shrimp and Artichoke Hearts, 78

Asparagus
Asparagus Tart, 188
Tomato-Topped Asparagus, 166
Ultimate Breakfast Strata, 84

Avocados
Avocado Salsa, 52
Grilled Portobello Mushrooms
   with Avocado and Goat
   Cheese, 190

Bacon
Bacon and Tomato Tarts, 163
Bacon-Wrapped Water
   Chestnuts, 78
BLT Dip, 24
Hot Bacon and Swiss
   Spread, 144

Beans. *See also* Green Beans
Curried Kidney Beans, 157
Jalapeño Black-Eyed Pea Dip, 152
Lentil and Lemon Soup, 118
Red and Chipotle Pepper
   Hummus, 53
Sugar Snap, Black Bean and
   Corn Sauté, 58

Beef
Flank Steak, 186
Grilled Beef Tenderloin
   Steaks, 33
Individual Beef Wellingtons with
   Mushroom Madeira Filling, 164
Italian Beef Sandwiches, 127
Larry's Steak Marinade, 186
Party Beef Tenderloin with
   Lime Horseradish Sauce, 76

Bell Peppers
Bell Pepper Risotto, 71
Five-Vegetable Slaw, 156
Grilled Pepper and
   Portobello Salad, 34
Red and Chipotle Pepper
   Hummus, 53
Spicy Red Bell Pepper Dip, 15

Beverages
Champagne Cocktails, 141
Coffee Bar, 140
Hotty-Toddy Toaster, 149
Little Jewels, 50
Old-Fashioned
   Lemonade, 29
Razmo, 32
Red Sangria, 50
Sparkling Iced Tea, 45
Spiked Spiced Cider, 126
Summer Wine, 117

Breads. *See also* Muffins
Broccoli Corn Bread, 193
Cheesy Artichoke
   Bread, 171
Cinnamon Roll-Ups, 87
Cream Cheese Danish, 88

Foolproof Homemade
    Yeast Rolls, 147
Garlic Bread, 175
Grilled Bread with
    Rosemary Butter, 73
Sour Cream Biscuits, 158

Breakfast/Brunch
Fresh Fruit Compote with
    Raspberry Cream, 90
Grits Galore, 85
Hot Brandied Fruit, 91
Mexican Green Chile
    Strata, 187
Sausage Stroganoff Over
    Grits, 86
Ultimate Breakfast Strata, 84

Broccoli
Asian Broccoli Wraps, 64
Broccoli Corn Bread, 193
Marinated Broccoli and
    Cauliflower, 80
Sweet-and-Sour Broccoli, 104

Cakes
Blueberry Pound Cake, 194
Glazed Almond Cake, 65
Grand Marnier Mousse
    Cake, 137
Lime Cake, 21
Mochaccino Cake, 148
Molten Chocolate Cakes with
    Mint Fudge Sauce, 105
Pink Lemonade Cake, 47
Pink Pound Cake, 28
Red Velvet Cake, 139
Sally's Famous Chocolate
    Cake, 197

Candy
Almond Toffee, 132
Chocolate Bag, 135
Coconut Balls, 133
Heath Bars, 195
Popcorn Treats, 111

Carrots
Carrot Soufflé, 43
Zesty Carrots, 19

Cheese. *See also* Swiss Cheese
Baked Corn Dip, 54
Baked Garlic and Sun-Dried
    Tomato Spread, 114
Bleu Cheese Iced Grapes, 79
Cheesy Mac n' Cheese, 109
Cheesy Shrimp and
    Grits Casserole, 172
Corinee's Cheese Straws, 24
Four-Cheese Pimento
    Sandwiches, 27
Garlic and Feta Spread, 27
Gourmet Potatoes, 189
Grilled Portobello Mushrooms
    with Avocado and Goat
    Cheese, 190
Italian Cheese Torta, 69
Kahlúa Pecan Brie, 16
Mexican Bread Bowl, 54
Mexican Green Chile Strata, 187
Olive Cups, 115
Red Delicious Cheese Spread, 40
Spinach Cheese Soup, 191
Warm Goat Cheese Toasts, 33

Cheesecakes
Herbed Cheesecake, 77
Pesto Chicken Cheesecake, 42

Chicken
Chicken Puffs, 182
Chicken Ribier, 179
Crunchy Chicken Salad, 25
Greek Chicken, 120
Green Chicken Enchiladas, 181
Hoisin Chicken Salad, 62
Honey Lime Grilled
    Chicken, 95
Hot Chicken and
    Sausage Dip, 171
Hot Chicken Salad, 180
Linguini with Chicken, Garlic
    and Mushrooms, 173
Oven-Baked Chicken Strips, 108
Pesto Chicken Cheesecake, 42
Rao's Chicken, 179

Chocolate
Chocolate Bag, 135
Chocolate Bread Pudding, 196
Chocolate Pâté, 81
Chocolate Sauce, 167
Coconut Balls, 133
German Sweet Chocolate Pies, 46
Grand Marnier Mousse
    Cake, 137
Heath Bars, 195
Mochaccino Cake, 148
Molten Chocolate Cakes with
    Mint Fudge Sauce, 105
Raspberry Fudge Finale, 167
Sally's Famous Chocolate
    Cake, 197

Cookies
Toffee Cookies, 29
Too-Good-to-Be-True
    Cookies, 111

Corn
Baked Corn Dip, 54
Crab and Corn-Filled Endive, 94
Crustless Corn Pie, 158
Grilled Corn with
Lime Butter, 72
Sugar Snap, Black Bean and
Corn Sauté, 58

Crab Meat
Crab and Corn-Filled
Endive, 94
Crab Cakes, 183

Cucumbers
Fresh Cucumber Salad, 26
Greek Salad, 120
Mexican Chopped Salad, 58
Summer's Bounty Salad, 72
Summer Wine, 117

Desserts. *See also* Cakes; Candy;
Cookies; Pies, Dessert;
Sauces, Dessert
Almond Cream-Filled
Strawberries, 80
Chocolate
Bread Pudding, 196
Chocolate Pâté, 81
Cinnamon Walnut Bread Pudding
with Whiskey Sauce, 159
Citrus Trifle, 123
Fruit Surprise, 193
Ice Cream Dessert, 194
Java Chip Parfait, 73
Layered Pumpkin Dessert, 129
Peppermint Whip, 134
Popcorn Treats, 111
Raspberry Fudge Finale, 167

Dips
Apple Dip, 153
Baked Corn Dip, 54
BLT Dip, 24
Cranberry Chutney, 144
Hot Chicken and
Sausage Dip, 171
Jalapeño Black-Eyed Pea Dip, 152
Mexican Bread Bowl, 54
Red and Chipotle Pepper
Hummus, 53
Spicy Red Bell Pepper Dip, 15

Egg Dishes
Asparagus Tart, 188
Mexican Green Chile Strata, 187
Not Your Momma's
Deviled Eggs, 26
Ultimate Breakfast Strata, 84

Enchiladas
Green Chicken Enchiladas, 181
Spinach Enchiladas with Sour
Cream Sauce, 56

Fish. *See also* Salmon
Baked Fish Fillets, 183
Macadamia-Crusted Grouper
with Peach and Mango
Salsa, 184
Sesame-Crusted Tuna Steaks, 103

Fruit. *See also* Apples; Avocados;
Pineapple; Strawberries
Autumn Salad with Pears, 128
Bleu Cheese Iced Grapes, 79
Blueberry Pound Cake, 194
Citrus Trifle, 123
Cranberry Chutney, 144

Five-Star Fruit Tart, 138
Fresh Fruit Compote with
Raspberry Cream, 90
Fruit Surprise, 193
Hot Brandied Fruit, 91
Peach and Mango Salsa, 185
Peach Salsa, 95

**Golfers and/or Their Wives'
Recipes**
Maria Floyd
Crab Cakes, 183
Fettuccine Alfredo, 176
Grilled Portobello Mushrooms
with Avocado and Goat
Cheese, 190
Rao's Chicken, 179
Charles Howell III
Cheesy Shrimp and Grits
Casserole, 172
Sally Irwin
Heath Bars, 195
Sally's Famous Chocolate
Cake, 197
**Mickelson Family Chef
David Long**
Garlic Bread, 175
Lobster Ravioli with Tomato
Tarragon Cream Sauce, 174
Bonnie Mize
Baked Fish Fillets, 183
Fruit Surprise, 193
Orange Blossoms, 89
Larry Mize
Larry's Steak Marinade, 186
Greg and Laura Norman
Macadamia-Crusted Grouper
with Peach and Mango
Salsa, 184

Barbara Nicklaus
Hot Chicken Salad, 180
Red Velvet Cake, 139
Rice Pilaf, 189
Arnold Palmer
Ice Cream Dessert, 194
Tomato and Onion
Salad, 190

Green Beans
Green Bean and Potato
Salad, 98
Speedy Green Beans, 110

Grilled Dishes
Cedar Plank Grilled Salmon, 70
Flank Steak, 186
Grilled Beef Tenderloin
Steaks, 33
Grilled Bread with
Rosemary Butter, 73
Grilled Corn with Lime Butter, 72
Grilled Pepper and
Portobello Salad, 34
Grilled Pineapple, 104
Grilled Portobello Mushrooms
with Avocado and Goat
Cheese, 190
Grilled Summer Vegetables
Over Orzo Pilaf, 96
Honey-Gingered Pork
Tenderloin, 17
Honey Lime Grilled
Chicken, 95
Larry's Steak Marinade, 186
Ribs with Honey Barbecue
Sauce, 155
You Thought You Didn't Like
Lamb Chops, 119

Grits
Cheesy Shrimp and
Grits Casserole, 172
Grits Galore, 85
Sausage Stroganoff Over
Grits, 86
Shrimp and Grits, 145

Lamb
You Thought You Didn't Like
Lamb Chops, 119

Lemonade
Lemonade Icebox Pie, 195
Old-Fashioned Lemonade, 29
Pink Lemonade Cake, 47

Meatless Main Dishes
Asparagus Tart, 188
Couscous-Stuffed Portobello
Mushrooms, 18
Fettuccine Alfredo, 176
Grilled Portobello Mushrooms
with Avocado and Goat
Cheese, 190
Herbed Cheesecake, 77
Pasta with Tomatoes and
Artichokes, 178
Spicy Sesame Noodles, 63
Spinach Squares, 44
Tomato Pie, 43

Muffins
Orange Blossoms, 89
Sweet Potato Muffins, 192

Mushrooms
Almond Raisin Rice, 121
Artichoke Salsa, 51

Couscous-Stuffed Portobello
Mushrooms, 18
Crostini with Mushrooms, 68
Grilled Pepper and
Portobello Salad, 34
Grilled Portobello Mushrooms
with Avocado and Goat
Cheese, 190
Linguini with Chicken, Garlic
and Mushrooms, 173
Mushroom Madeira Filling, 165
Rice Pilaf, 189
Sausage Stroganoff
Over Grits, 86
Spinach Enchiladas with
Sour Cream Sauce, 56

Nuts. *See also* Almonds; Peanuts;
Pecans; Walnuts
Italian Cheese Torta, 69
Macadamia-Crusted Grouper with
Peach and Mango Salsa, 184

Pasta
Cheesy Mac 'n Cheese, 109
Fettuccine Alfredo, 176
Grilled Summer Vegetables
Over Orzo Pilaf, 96
Linguini with Chicken, Garlic
and Mushrooms, 173
Lobster Ravioli in Tomato
Tarragon Cream Sauce, 174
Pasta with Tomatoes and
Artichokes, 178
Spicy Sesame Noodles, 63

Peanuts
Boiled Peanuts, 154
Popcorn Treats, 111

Pecans
Autumn Salad with Pears, 128
Cranberry Chutney, 144
Cream Cheese Pecan Pie, 99
German Sweet Chocolate Pies, 46
Lemon Bites, 136
Olive Cups, 115
Raspberry Fudge Finale, 167
Red Delicious Cheese Spread, 40

Pies, Dessert
Caramel Walnut Pie with
    Port Wine Cherries, 37
Cream Cheese Pecan Pie, 99
Five-Star Fruit Tart, 138
German's Sweet Chocolate Pies, 46
Lemonade Icebox Pie, 195
Lemon Bites, 136
Strawberry Margarita Pie, 59

Pies, Savory
Asparagus Tart, 188
Bacon and Tomato Tarts, 163
Crustless Corn Pie, 158
Tomato Pie, 43

Pineapple
Cranberry Chutney, 144
Grilled Pineapple, 104
Tangy Apple Salad, 110

Pork. *See also* Bacon; Sausage
Honey-Gingered Pork
    Tenderloin, 17
Mexican Pulled Pork
    Over Yellow Rice, 55
Ribs with Honey Barbecue
    Sauce, 155
Slow-Cooker Barbecue, 154

Potatoes
Gourmet Potatoes, 189
Granddad's Potato Soup, 126
Green Bean and Potato Salad, 98
Lemon Horseradish
    New Potatoes, 35

Poultry. *See* Chicken

Restaurant Recipes
Chicken Ribier, 179
Fried Green Tomatoes with
    Rémoulade Sauce, 102
Grand Marnier Mousse Cake, 137
Green Chicken Enchiladas, 181
Molten Chocolate Cakes with
    Mint Fudge Sauce, 105
Oyster and Artichoke Soup, 162
Sesame-Crusted Tuna Steaks, 103

Rice
Almond Raisin Rice, 121
Bell Pepper Risotto, 71
Mexican Pulled Pork
    Over Yellow Rice, 55
Rice Pilaf, 189

Salads
Autumn Salad with Pears, 128
Balsamic Bermuda Onion
    Salad, 146
Bok Choy Salad, 64
Crunchy Chicken Salad, 25
Five-Vegetable Slaw, 156
Fresh Cucumber Salad, 26
Fruity Spinach Salad with
    Honey Poppy Seed Dressing, 97
Greek Salad, 120
Green Bean and Potato Salad, 98

Green Jacket House Salad, 41
Grilled Pepper and Portobello
    Salad, 34
Hoisin Chicken Salad, 62
Hot Chicken Salad, 180
Marinated Broccoli and
    Cauliflower, 80
Marinated Garden Salad, 20
Mexican Chopped Salad, 58
Summer's Bounty Salad, 72
Tangy Apple Salad, 110
Tomato and Onion Salad, 190

Salmon
Cedar Plank Grilled
    Salmon, 70
Salmon Roll-Ups, 79

Salsa
Artichoke Salsa, 51
Avocado Salsa, 52
Peach and Mango Salsa, 185
Peach Salsa, 95
Tomato Chow-Chow, 128
Traditional Salsa, 52

Sandwiches
Asian Broccoli Wraps, 64
Four-Cheese Pimento
    Sandwiches, 27
Italian Beef Sandwiches, 127
Slow-Cooker Barbecue, 154

Sauces, Dessert
Chocolate Sauce, 167
Mint Fudge Sauce, 105

Sauces, Savory
Cranberry Chutney, 144

Creamy Shrimp and
    Sausage Sauce, 177
Honey Barbecue Sauce, 155
Lime Horseradish Sauce, 76
Pesto, 42
Rémoulade Sauce, 102
Sour Cream Sauce, 57
Tomato Chow-Chow, 128
Tomato Tarragon Cream
    Sauce, 174

Sausage
Creamy Shrimp and
    Sausage Sauce, 177
Hot Chicken and Sausage Dip, 171
Sausage Stroganoff Over Grits, 86
Ultimate Breakfast Strata, 84

Scallops
Scallop Shooters in
    Saffron Cream, 116
Seared Scallops with
    Lemon and Dill, 170

Seafood. *See also* Crab Meat; Fish;
    Salmon; Scallops; Shrimp
Lobster Ravioli in Tomato
    Tarragon Cream Sauce, 174
Oyster and Artichoke Soup, 162

Shrimp
Cheesy Shrimp and
    Grits Casserole, 172
Creamy Shrimp and
    Sausage Sauce, 177
Mustard-Marinated Shrimp, 14
Shrimp and Artichoke
    Hearts, 78
Shrimp and Grits, 145

Soups
Granddad's Potato Soup, 126
Lentil and Lemon Soup, 118
Oyster and Artichoke
    Soup, 162
Spinach Cheese Soup, 191

Spinach
Artichoke Spinach Pinwheels, 122
Fruity Spinach Salad with
    Honey Poppy Seed Dressing, 97
Spinach Cheese Soup, 191
Spinach Enchiladas with
    Sour Cream Sauce, 56
Spinach Squares, 44

Spreads
Baked Garlic and Sun-Dried
    Tomato Spread, 114
Garlic and Feta Spread, 27
Hot Bacon and Swiss Spread, 144
Italian Cheese Torta, 69
Pesto, 42
Red and Chipotle Pepper
    Hummus, 53
Red Delicious Cheese Spread, 40

Strawberries
Almond Cream-Filled
    Strawberries, 80
Citrus Trifle, 123
Fruity Spinach Salad with
    Honey Poppy Seed Dressing, 97
Pink Pound Cake, 28
Strawberry Margarita Pie, 59

Swiss Cheese
Hot Bacon and Swiss Spread, 144
Spinach Cheese Soup, 191

Tomatoes
Artichoke Salsa, 51
Avocado Salsa, 52
Bacon and Tomato Tarts, 163
Baked Garlic and Sun-Dried
    Tomato Spread, 114
Fried Green Tomatoes with
    Rémoulade Sauce, 102
Mexican Chopped Salad, 58
Pasta with Tomatoes and
    Artichokes, 178
Summer's Bounty Salad, 72
Tomato and Onion Salad, 190
Tomato Chow-Chow, 128
Tomato Pie, 43
Tomato Poppers, 32
Tomato Tarragon Cream
    Sauce, 174
Tomato-Topped Asparagus, 166
Traditional Salsa, 52

Vegetables. *See* Artichokes;
    Asparagus; Beans; Bell Peppers;
    Broccoli; Carrots; Corn;
    Cucumbers; Green Beans;
    Mushrooms; Potatoes;
    Spinach; Tomatoes
Brussels Sprouts with Pancetta, 36
Grilled Summer Vegetables
    Over Orzo Pilaf, 96

Walnuts
Caramel Walnut Pie with
    Port Wine Cherries, 37
Cinnamon Walnut Bread Pudding
    with Whiskey Sauce, 159

Junior League of Augusta, Georgia

P.O. Box 40058
Augusta, Georgia 30909
Order online at www.jlaugusta.org, or
call 888-JLT-TIME or 706-733-9098

Name _____

Address _____

City _____ State _____ Zip _____

Telephone _____ Email _____

Quantity		Total
_____	*Par 3, Tea-Time at the* MASTERS® at $21.95 per book	$ _____
_____	*Tea-Time at the* MASTERS® at $18.95 per book	$ _____
_____	*Second Round, Tea-Time at the* MASTERS® at $16.95 per book	$ _____
_____	Purchase all three for $51.95 per set	$ _____
_____	Gift Wrap (Optional) at $1.00 per book	$ _____
	Subtotal	$ _____
	Shipping and handling at $4.00 for first book; $3.00 for each additional book	$ _____
	Georgia residents add 7% sales tax	$ _____
	Total	$ _____

Method of Payment: [   ] MasterCard   [   ] VISA
                    [   ] Check enclosed payable to Tea-Time Publications

Account Number _____ Expiration Date _____

Signature _____

Please photocopy this page.